SELF-CATERING IN
ITALY

OTHER SELF-CATERING GUIDES
PUBLISHED BY CHRISTOPHER HELM

Self-catering in Portugal
Carol Wright

Self-catering in Greece, Mainland and Islands
Florica Kyriacopoulos and Tim Salmon

Self-catering in Spain
Carole Stewart with Chris Stewart

Self-catering in France
Arthur and Barbara Eperon

Self-catering Afloat
Bill Glenton

SELF-CATERING IN
ITALY

Making the most of local food and drink

Susan Grossman

CHRISTOPHER HELM
London

For Emily
whose favourite food is pasta!

© 1987 Susan Grossman
Christopher Helm (Publishers) Ltd, Imperial House,
21-25 North Street, Bromley, Kent BR1 1SD
Line drawings by Mike Dodd

British Library Cataloguing in Publication Data

Grossman, Susan
    Self-catering in Italy: making the most
    of local food and drink.
    1. Cookery, Italian   2. Beverages —
    Italy
    I. Title
    641'.0945   TX723

    ISBN 0-7470-1204-0

Typeset in Souvenir by Leaper & Gard Ltd, Bristol, England
Printed and bound in the Channel Islands by
The Guernsey Press Co. Ltd, Guernsey, Channel Islands

Contents

Acknowledgements

I would like to thank the following people for their help in compiling this book: Federica Bellici at the Italian State Tourist Office, Kathleen and Philip Sheriden at Magic of Italy, Jill Goolden for her invaluable advice on Italian wine and Vanessa della Torre for contributions to the recipes. Many thanks also to Signor Bifulco, Italian butcher, and I. Camisa, delicatessan in Old Compton Street, Soho and to John Cavaciuti cheese and pasta specialist in South End Green, Hampstead.

The Regions of Italy

1

Introduction

This is not a book about how to become an expert Italian cook in the space of a holiday fortnight, but how to make the time you spend eating in Italy as much of an adventure as the rest of your holiday.

Just as you'll probably be wanting to discover the best beaches, the best sights to see, perhaps the best places to get away from it all, with this guide you should also discover the best way to eat well too — whether you are doing all the cooking yourself or eating out in restaurants.

Italian shops, supermarkets and markets can be a bit daunting at first, what with Latin hysteria and the language problem. Trying to explain to a butcher that you want him to flatten your veal escalope is no mean feat if your Italian extends only as far as asking for a *cappuccino*. Even if you can manage the language there's the problem of what to do with the food when you get it home. Nobody, it seems to me, would want to spend valuable holiday time checking recipes or slaving over a hot stove.

Italian food has a rather limited reputation outside Italy. A lot of people think that Italians exist on nothing but pasta, pizza, ice-cream and veal escalopes. They couldn't be more wrong. Italians claim almost as many (if not more) cheeses than France, produce *more* wine than any other country in the world, and their fruit, vegetables, fish and seafood are as good as any you'll find anywhere else on the Continent.

As for recipes, the exciting thing about Italy is that not only does every region have its own unique specialities but each also does something different with the same basic produce, which means that travelling about is a gastronomic adventure. With this guide you can try food from different regions, *wherever* you are. For example, in the north around Bologna dishes tend to be richer than in most other regions with the

1

accent on creamy sauces, home-made pastas and heavy stews. In the centre of Italy in Tuscany, they prefer to keep things simple, while in the south they're fond of adding tomatoes, anchovies, garlic, peppers and black olives to a lot of dishes.

Whenever you go to Italy you can enjoy produce that hasn't yet appeared in the shops at home — and a lot that never gets out of the country. The further south you go the earlier the season begins. By May you can already get sweet juicy peaches, cherries, melons, lemons and oranges. A lot of regions spend the summer bottling up their mushrooms and aubergines/eggplant, tomatoes and peppers in olive oil, ready to eat in the winter months. They also preserve their fruit in alcohol.

Unlike French cooking, Italian cooking is basically straightforward. The Italians don't go in much for elaborate sauces and complicated ways of preparing food. They rely on the best fresh ingredients available which they buy on the day they want to use them. There is simply no need for elaborate sauces, except, of course, for pasta.

When they are stuck for ideas, Italian women don't so much consult cookery books as each other. They exchange recipes in much the same way as children exchange jokes. And, of course, pass them down through generations. Italians also eat and enjoy all sorts of things we wouldn't dream of trying: they quite happily put a calf's head in a stew, for example, or in cities eat tripe sandwiches off a stall in the street for lunch. Most of all they are proud of their food, get terribly upset if you don't like a dish in a restaurant and go out of their way to be helpful in markets if you don't recognise something.

Mass production is another matter. Until about ten years ago Italy could have been accused of taking a rather uncaring attitude to some of its produce — much of its wine was dumped in the European wine lake, unnecessary additives were added to foods like ice-cream. Almost anything went into sausages and salami. These days they've cleaned up their act a lot. Food laws are much stricter and closely adhered to and Italians are very aware of the importance of nutrition. They are much stricter than we are, for example, about the preservatives they allow to be added to cooked meats, and babyfoods.

The beauty of making your own meals on an Italian holiday is that you don't actually have to *cook* very much. You can buy so much delicious food ready to eat from *alimentari*, *salumeria* or *rosticceria*. My favourite Italian foods don't need cooking at all! Two weeks' worth of Parma ham and melon, platefuls of tomato with slices of *mozzarella*, salads made up of whatever's seasonal in the market: tomatoes, fresh basil, raw fennel, or red *radicchio*, raw ham and salami, fresh *pecorino* cheese, a few olives or anchovies and, of course, good olive oil and local bread. How long does it take to grill or gently fry a few prawns, a thick wedge of swordfish or a tender piece of veal? Add some fresh sage, a squeeze of lemon and serve it outside in the shade with a cold bottle of wine. For dessert choose the morning's white-fleshed peaches, cherries or strawberries or buy an unfamiliar flavour of ice-cream and keep it in the freezer. It's easy to have memorable meals in Italy.

Holiday cooking *should* be easy, fun and different from cooking at home. The recipe section at the back of the book should give you some ideas as to what Italians do with their food. Even if all you do on holiday is to try out a few of them in your kitchen and sample some unfamiliar dishes in restaurants, you can't fail to have extended your Italian repertoire by the time you get home.

What better place to practise cooking Italian food than in the land of olive oil and *mozzarella*, Parma ham and pasta.

2
HOW TO
USE THIS
BOOK

The chapter on 'Shopping in Italy' should help you get your bearings in terms of knowing what to buy where. Then, although it doesn't really matter *where* in Italy you're holidaying the chapter on 'The Different Regions' will tell you what Italians in different parts of Italy prepare in their kitchens. Since almost all the ingredients are available all over the country you can try out virtually everything, although obviously there will be seasonal availabilities. If some of the dishes seem a bit too ambitious for holiday cooking you can always look out for them in the local restaurants or have a go when you get home.

Nobody's suggesting for a minute that you have to spend *every* evening at the kitchen sink!

The next chapters deal with specific foods and ingredients (meat, fish, cheese, staples, fruit, vegetables, etc.). They should help you identify produce that's perhaps not available outside Italy — like herbs, certain cheeses, vegetables or fruit. They should also make shopping a bit easier; for example, Italian cuts of meat are very different from ours.

Next there is a chapter on pasta, a bit about the different types, and what Italians do with them and how to make your own, then a brief look at bread — which is rated very highly, and pizza.

Italians may not go in for puddings, but cakes, biscuits, ice-cream and sweets need a chapter to themselves. While you probably won't want to attempt making some of the more elaborate cakes yourself, the chapter might make you more adventurous in trying out what you see in the shops.

As for wines, Italians produce a larger number of wines than France — and that's without all the aperitifs and liqueurs — if you're planning on doing any serious drinking you might as well buy the best wines, some of which never leave the country.

Since you're almost certainly not going to spend your entire time cooking, the chapter on 'Eating and Drinking Out' should ensure you get the best out of Italian bars and restaurants. I've explained menus, covered popular snacks and how to avoid paying twice as much as you need to.

There's a chapter too on special diets, including some tips on keeping children happy, and 'What to Take with You' — or rather what not to.

The glossary includes words I think might come in handy, weights and measures to help you convert and recipes — a sort of random selection of things I like to eat and things you might enjoy making! You don't have to try all of them on holiday — save some for cheering up a rainy day at home when you get back.

3

SHOPPING
IN ITALY

Shopping in Italy is fun, especially in the markets. You should try to have the correct amount as there is a chronic shortage of small change. If shopkeepers have no small change they may give you sweets or a telephone *gettone* instead.

You don't really need to speak much Italian as all you have to do is point. In markets stallholders are generally very friendly and helpful. If you're buying hams or cheeses they will almost always let you have a little taste before you buy. Weights are in kilos but there's never any pressure to buy a full kilo if you don't want to, a couple of peaches are fine.

Because shops are open late you don't have to eat away into valuable holiday time doing the shopping, but if you do want the freshest fruit and vegetables, meat or fish it's well worth getting up early in the morning to go to the market. Italian housewives don't make themselves long lists for pre-planned menus, they just go along and buy whatever takes their fancy.

SHOP HOURS

In summer most shops open at 8.00a.m., shut between 1.00p.m. and 4.00p.m. and open again until 8.00p.m. Seven in the evening always seems to be the busiest time with Italian families out in force, including babes in arms. Half day closing varies but is often Monday morning or Thursday afternoon. In winter the *siesta* is shorter and shops close at about 7.00p.m.

You cannot bargain in shops. The price is fixed, although occasionally you can get a discount for paying with traveller's cheques. Prices for food are fixed in markets, too, so you cannot bargain, although you can bargain for things like bags or shoes.

7

BANKS

Leave yourself a lot of time or go first thing in the morning. Italian bank queues either never seem to move or you end up in the wrong one and have to start all over again. Banks will cash traveller's cheques and Eurocheques. Security is very strict. At some banks they have introduced entry through a cylindrical glass booth. You press a button and one side opens, letting you in. It then closes and you are let out inside the bank. Great fun — a bit like being beamed up to another planet!

Banks open at 8.30 a.m. and shut at about 1.00 p.m. They may open again at 2.30 p.m. until 3.30 p.m. Monday to Friday. In small places they may have shorter hours. Outside these hours you can change money at *Uffici Cambio* or in hotels but the rate will not be as good.

SHOPS

Baker (*panettiere, panificio, fornaio*)

Bakers sell fresh bread and rolls usually baked on the premises. You can also buy thick breadsticks (*grissini*) and some bakers will also sell slices of cooked pizza, freshly made pasta (and pizza dough), breadcrumbs and home-made biscuits and cakes. You buy your hot brioche, or *cornetto* in the south, rolls and croissants for breakfast in local bars. You may also be able to get *focaccia*, bread soaked in olive oil and salt and seasoned with herbs or onions — often these are filled with ham or cheese. If there isn't a baker's shop the *alimentari* will sell bread and filled rolls.

Butcher (*macelleria*)

In small towns or villages the local butcher slaughters his own meat and sells it a day later, which usually means you're not going to get a fantastic choice. You may see a whole side of beef or a kid hanging in his shop, perhaps a few pheasants, a tray of tripe and a big lump of liver or veal on a marble slab. Meat is priced depending on the cut (first, second and third quality). It is best to tell the butcher what you are planning to cook and he will give you what you need. When it is hot there won't be much on display. Salamis and hams are sold in *alimentari* or *salumeria*, and chickens and rabbits are often sold in separate shops.

Cake Shop (*pasticceria*)

An Italian *pasticceria* is not the sort of place you can walk past without going in! The cakes in the window are often a lot more elaborate and rich looking than those in French patisseries or continental bakeries here — gigantic *Monte Bianco*, a chestnut dessert smothered in chocolate and cream, rich cakes layered with chocolate and nuts, meringue, *zabaglione* sponges — all about six inches high! They don't just sell cakes. Inside there will be counters of tiny hand-made biscuits often made with almonds, marzipan beautifully moulded into fruit or figurines, trays of home-made chocolates, crystallised fruits, sugared almonds, marron glaces ...

At Easter there will be boxes of *Colomba* cake all over the place, at Christmas huge boxes of *Panettone*. Many *pasticceria* also sell home-made ice-cream (in flavours you'll probably never have heard of) and they may also have a few round tables and an *espresso* machine so you can indulge yourself immediately!

Chemist (*farmacia*)

Pharmacies usually have a green or red cross outside. They dispense drugs from prescriptions. They don't go in for a wide range of shampoos and perfumes (there are special shops that only sell perfume) but sell medicines and ointments, babyfoods and toys and a small range of toiletries, over the counter. The pharmacist may speak some English and is a useful person to consult for minor aches and pains. Though watch out for ointments and drugs with a bit of everything in them, in the hope that one of the ingredients might work!

Cheese Shop (*casa del formaggio*)

These, of course, specialise in cheeses, usually the local ones as well as *mozzarella* and Parmesan. You'll see enormous rounds of Parmesan stacked up; you buy a wedge to grate yourself. There will be bowls full of soft fresh cheeses, and *mozzarella* swimming in its own whey. You may also be able to buy hams and ready made pasta dishes, jars of *antipasto*, fruit juices, milk, dried mushrooms and much the same produce as in an *alimentari*.

Dairy (*latteria*)

Not every town has one, but most villages do. A *latteria* will sell cheese, milk, cream, yoghurt and butter, and anything else the owner feels like stocking.

Delicatessen (*alimentari, salumeria*)

Although Italians do use large supermarkets a great deal

most prefer to do serious food shopping in their local *alimentari* or *salumeria*. Usually it's as much of a social occasion as a shopping expedition, with gossip and news exchanged over the counter.

Salumeria and *alimentari* sell the same sort of things, except that a *salumeria* sells more hams and cooked meats, while an *alimentari* will usually also sell baby products, cakes, cheeses and soap powder. What you can't see will be stacked up in boxes at the back.

The name doesn't matter much; you'll spot the local deli a mile off; its window should be full of tempting foods. They are often quite dark and cramped inside and every available space will be packed with food: the ceiling strung with hams and sausages, boxes of *Colomba* cake at Easter or *Panforte* at Christmas; the counter will have trays of freshly made pasta or home-made cakes, bowls of thick *mascarpone* cream, or crystallised fruit. On the shelves will be sealed jars of *antipasto* in oil; perhaps seafood or squid, artichoke hearts and peppers. There will be a drum of anchovies, perhaps a few stiff slabs of dried cod, bags of dried mushrooms and herbs, wines, olive oil, bright red tins of *Amaretto di Saronno* biscuits, Lavazza coffee and jar upon jar of pasta sauces (*pesto* with clams, *ragu*). Choose well-known brands like Barilla, Sacla, Polli or Cirio and you can't go far wrong.

Avoid those empty, quiet *alimentari* which have a dried up piece of ham or cheese sharing a counter with some shoelaces or a tin of peas. Try to shop where the locals go.

Fruit Shop (*fruttivendolo*)

Most of the fruit and vegetables will be piled up outside the shop and you may be able to help yourself (you will be given a basket) and then take it inside to be weighed. You may not find a very big selection. If you can, find a local market.

Markets (*mercato*)

Outside big towns you will usually find a local market open one day a week. It may just consist of a few stalls selling fruit, plastic shoes and children's toys, or it may cram every side street and sell food as well as everything else under the sun. Markets usually start early in the morning and pack up at about noon. As well as fresh fruit, herbs and vegetables grown by local farmers, you will be able to buy good local cheeses, olive oil, meat, roast chickens on spits, hams, salamis and cheap household utensils. You can usually get very good discounts for bulk purchases, particularly trays of fruit and you may be given a basket to fill up yourself, although stall-holders don't usually object if you buy just one piece of fruit. In bigger towns markets are often daily and there will usually be a special covered area for selling meat and poultry. If you're by the sea the fish market is usually by the port. Even if you don't buy anything, just wandering around an Italian market is an experience. Worth going out of your way for is Venice's fish market and the market at Padua which spreads out under coloured awnings on either side of Il Salone.

Post Office (*ufficio postale*)

Look for PT signs. Most post offices are open from 8.15 a.m. in the morning until 1.00 or 2.00 p.m. Monday to Friday with a half day on Saturday. You buy your stamps (*francobolli*) at *tabaccaio* (tobacconists) with a T sign outside them, and incidentally your salt too as it is a state monopoly. There are international call boxes for long distance calls. For local calls you can also pay with *gettone* (special coins). Since there is a chronic shortage of small change you will often get them whether you want them or not. Otherwise the *tabaccaio* will supply them.

Rosticceria

Rosticceria almost all have a spit in the window roasting a chicken or some other meat, basting it regularly with garlic or herbs. A *rosticceria* is the place to head for if you haven't prepared dinner or are on the way out for the day and want to take a picnic with you. As well as roast meats they also sell a wide range of ready cooked dishes to take away or to eat there. You can usually buy trays of *lasagne*, chips, potato croquettes, russian salad and *suppli*, rice croquettes stuffed with *mozzarella* and mincemeat.

Supermarkets (*supermercato*)

Supermarkets are in all towns, large and small. They sell much the same range of products as ours do. Many have fruit on stands outside the shop and a good deli counter (but not as good as an *alimentari*).

You'll see all sorts of familiar brands and Italian ones too. If you insist on Kellogg's cornflakes (they sell Weetabix and Cocopops too) they'll be a lot dearer than at home. As far as feeding the family is concerned, the only thing you might have trouble obtaining is orange squash. The Italians go in for cans and bottles of fizzy drinks, fresh unsweetened juices, or those sweetened (but delicious) thick peach, pear and apricot juices sold in small bottles and jars. You'll also be offered several varieties of bottled water.

Look out for quick and easy packets. Italians make life simple, if you don't fancy cooking, by producing ready-made pizza mixes, cartons and jars of sauces for spaghetti. You can even buy *besciamella* (béchamel) for *lasagne*. They sell every conceivable shape and size of dried pasta.

Frozen foods are worth considering too. Findus do things we never see here. Try *bocconcini di mozzarella impareti* (fried *mozzarella* balls that melt in the middle when you heat them up), fish dishes, like *frittura mista* (fried pieces of fish), *zuppa di pesce* (fish soup), *vongole* (clams) and ready-made pizza dough.

You can buy all your household needs in supermarkets; they are often open quite late, will deliver and they stock babyfoods and toiletries, although pharmacies have a better selection.

SHOPPING

Baker	*Panettiere, panificio, fornaio*
Butcher	*Macelleria*
Cake shop	*Pasticceria*
Cheese shop	*Casa del formaggio*
Chemist	*Farmacia*
Dairy	*Latteria*
Delicatessen	*Alimentari, salumeria*
Doctor	*Medico, ambulatorio*
Exchange Bureau/ *Bureau de Change*	*Uffici Cambio*
Fish shop	*Pescheria*
General grocer	*Alimentari*
Greengrocer	*Fruttivendolo*
Ice-cream shop	*Gelateria*
Market	*Mercato*
Newsagent	*Giornalaio*
Off licence/Liquor store	*Enoteca, negozio di vini, e liquori*
Pharmacy	*Farmacia*
Post office	*Ufficio postale*
Cooked food	*Rosticceria*
Supermarket	*Supermercato*
Tobacconist	*Tabaccaio*

4

THE
DIFFERENT
REGIONS

Wherever you're staying in Italy, you'll find a large number of regional specialities. Italians are quite possessive about certain dishes and recipes have been handed down over generations. Although a lot of dishes have been adopted by other regions (some even escape abroad) there are a number that only appear on their home territory.

Another way to find out what local Italians do with the produce that's available in the markets is to look at a few restaurant menus. Actually, looking may not be enough; you may have to do a bit of sampling.

I've divided the chapter into regions (grouping a few together). If you're not sure which region you're going to I've listed some of the main resorts at the top. You should be able to see quite easily what each has to offer in the way of dishes, but since a lot of the basic ingredients are available all over Italy it might be worth your while reading the entries for regions you're *not* visiting too. Although you may find them on restaurant menus (usually simpler places away from the main tourist areas), the idea is to give you some ideas for preparing food yourself. You'll find quite few regional recipes in the section at the back of the book. And remember you don't have to follow rigidly the quantities or the ingredients — Italians certainly don't.

ABRUZZI AND MOLISE

Pescara, Alba Adriatica, Teramo, L'Aquila, Giulianova, Silvi Marina, Francavilla, Vasto and Montesilvano — apart from Pescara you probably won't have heard of any of these places. Both regions are in the centre of Italy and border the Adriatic. Inland, the highest peaks of the Apennines have

13

thickly forested slopes, and villages are famous for their handicrafts, particularly their hand-hammered copper pots (*cotturo*) which are used to cook lamb using herbs from the woods. Neither are regions that attract many visitors. A rare breed of Marsican bear lurks in the National Park of Abruzzi — perhaps that's why.

The Abruzzi is one of the most rigidly traditional as far as cooking is concerned and it produces many a master chef, most of which are from the same family.

In most kitchens you'll find a strange looking gadget called a *chitarra*, a sort of wooden loom with steel cords, not much more than a foot high. When plucked it makes a sound like a musical instrument, yet it's used to make *maccheroni alla chitarra* the most characteristic dish of the region served with a meat, usually lamb sauce, or *pecorino* cheese and tomato. They also like ravioli stuffed with *ricotta*, thick vegetable soups (made with cardoons, lentils and wild chicory) and tiny cheese and herb omelettes.

Most pasta dishes are accompanied by the sauce made from stewed meat which is served dry as a main course. A lot of meat dishes are quite spicy, and flavoured with hot chillies, peppers and sometimes saffron and garlic. Pork is the meat eaten most frequently; lamb and kid are roasted whole over coals; the internal organs of animals are made into *budelline* sausages, and *fegati dolci*, pork liver sausages with honey.

Along the coast, mullet is boned and stuffed, you'll find squid, cuttlefish, sardines and sole often cooked on the grill or prepared with tomato, and sweet and sharp peppers. Sometimes fish is pickled and preserved in vinegar after being quickly fried.

Inland sheep produce various kinds of *pecorino* cheese.

Sweets to look for include *torrone* from L'Aquila, *torrone* with figs from Chieti and *confetti* made in all colours and put together in garlands and flowers from Sulmona. *Caggiunitti* are cakes filled with chestnut purée and chickpeas. *Parrozzo* is a honey and almond cake covered with chocolate. The Centerbe liqueur, made with herbs, is also from the region.

In Molise they cook simply on the open grill: lamb, pork, kid and mountain beef, using terracotta pots to simmer spicy sauces and stews containing peppers, Pastas may have a kid sauce. The rivers produce trout, carp, tench and shrimp. There are good cheeses; and most of the sweets, as in the Abruzzi, contain liberal amounts of mountain honey.

APULIA (PUGLIA)

Torre Canne, Selva di Fasano, Tremiti Islands, Rosa Marina, Lecce, Foggia, Bari, Brindisi, Taranto and the Gargano peninsula, an area of great natural beauty, all comprise Apulia (Puglia), Italy's heel, which, in addition, has some magnificent beaches backed by fantastic caves. Inland is a barren stony landscape of fields surrounded by low stone walls out of which grow curious stone constructions (*trulli* and dolmen). Apulia has one of the richest agricultures in Italy; the best wheat (for making pasta), olive oil from Lecce (where the trees grow to huge proportions), excellent grapes and large quantities of fruit and hot-house vegetables.

As well as vineyards and rows of olive trees you'll see figs and almonds and plenty of herbs and berries growing wild.

There is little meat eaten in Apulia, although there are some pork dishes, and rabbit is cooked with capers (*coniglio ai capperi*).

Along the coast oysters are cultivated at Taranto and are excellent; mullet is cooked in paper; sea bream are cooked over an open fire; anchovies are fried with lots of oregano; mussels go into a soup with white wine and tomatoes (*zuppa di cozze*) and you can get lobster from the Ionian and Tremiti Islands.

Pasta is really the staple diet, served with numerous sauces made with fish or little shellfish, lamb or pork. You mop them up with some of the best bread in Italy, giant loaves baked in wood burning stoves. Bread is also eaten with olive oil, tomatoes and onions.

The markets will be full of vegetables. It's quite easy to make the Apulian dish, *capriata*, a purée of fresh broad beans, chicory, bitter wild onions (*lampasciuni*) and olive oil.

For dessert there are melons, peaches, grapes and figs, the latter often being spiced and baked in the oven.

Apulia's wine production is enormous and wines are strong, so are the bitter liqueurs made with herbs, walnuts and almonds.

CALABRIA AND BASILICATA

Scalea, Crotone, Soverato, Diamante, Scilla, Cetraro, Copanello, Praia a Mare, Maratea, Matera and Reggio Calabria make up Calabria and Basilicata. Calabria is Italy's most southern mainland region, the boot, a short kick away from Sicily. These two regions are the poorest in Italy.

In Basilicata the mountains stretch right down to the sea and the coastline is relatively inaccessible. Inland, wolves still roam in the forests. It is not a region many tourists visit.

Calabria, on the other hand, is becoming more popular. It is roughly the size of Wales. Most of it is mountainous and is separated from Sicily by the Straits of Messina. The coastline is some 500 miles long and there are good beaches and resorts with the Tyrrhenian Sea on one side and the Ionian on the other. The narrowest part is only 30 miles across. Until a few years ago few tourists ventured this far. But with new airports and good roads the region has become a lot more accessible. Apart from Reggio Calabria (from where boats leave for Sicily) there are few big towns.

The Ionian coast is the most attractive with lots of rocky bays and some very good beaches. The sea is turquoise blue. On the other coast the beaches are grey and pebbly and it is more built up. Beware, it becomes very, very hot in mid-summer.

The cooking in Calabria reflects the different landscapes; the mountains, which rise to 5000 feet, the countryside and the coast. It is basically simple fare, not dissimilar from the food you get around Naples.

The mountain slopes are covered in olive trees, chestnuts, pines and flowering rhododendrons. There is game and small wild mushrooms. Further down you'll smell jasmine, oregano, rosemary and fennel — many growing by the roadside. There are lemon trees everywhere and the bergamot tree also grows in the region; Calabria has a world monopoly on the perfume and skin lotions made from it.

Hot red peppers and olives dominate the cooking. The olive trees grow to gigantic proportions, and olives drop to the ground to be picked up and made into a fairly heavy olive oil. In autumn, peppers are hung out to dry outside the houses, stretched out on washing lines between trees. You may see them for sale, scattered in trays by the roadside like a brilliant red carpet. Peppers are used in the region's *salame*; watch out for the bright red (hot) *morsello* sausage.

Aubergines/eggplant are just as prolific as peppers and an originally Calabrian dish, *melanzane alla parmigiana* (see p. 147) is now eaten all over Italy and abroad too. You can buy jars of aubergines/eggplant pickled in oil.

Sauces for pastas (which come in all shapes and sizes), pork, lamb and freshwater fish are most commonly made with aubergines/eggplant, tomatoes, garlic, oregano and mint, *pecorino* cheese is sprinkled on top.

Vegetables are used to make soups (*licurda* is made with broad beans, *zuppa di cipolle* with onions). Red onions are also roasted.

Along the coast, markets will be full of anchovies to cook with lemon juice, fresh sardines to grill with olive oil and oregano and, as in Sicily, tuna and swordfish which are cut into steaks and often cooked with capers and olives.

There is little meat, but you may get pork and if you're lucky kid or lamb.

Fresh fruit includes oranges and lemons, apricots, prunes and figs which are stuffed with walnuts. Nuts and fruits are dried in the sun or in ovens. Elaborate desserts are based on dried fruits. There are plenty of cheeses: *ricotta, caciocavalli, pecorino* (there's even one with peppers). Sweets play an important part in the region's many festivals, try the *torrone gelato*, and *taralli*.

Wines are strong and most of them red.

Basilicata's offerings are similar except that since it has little coast, most of its produce comes from the mountains (try the ham) and woods, lakes and rivers. You'll get trout and eel, wild boar and hare. They prefer chillies to pepper, and hot spicy sausages are referred to all over Italy as *basilicata*. Of the pasta dishes, one worth seeking out is *manate*, an entire dish made by hand from one strand of spaghetti.

Of the sweets, try *cuccia* made with walnuts and pomegranate seeds, *cicirata* made with pasta and honey and *panzerotti* made with chick pea cream. Figs, walnuts and chestnuts are good too.

CAMPANIA

Sorrento, Positano, Amalfi, Ravello, Minori, Maiori, Palinuro, Vietri sul Mare, Santa Maria and San Marco di Castellabate, Baia Domizia, Capri, Ischia and Naples. Campania is the land of pasta, pizza, ice-cream, *mozzarella* cheese and dishes cooked *alla Napoletana* with a tomato sauce.

The Bay of Naples has been attracting visitors for longer than most other parts of Europe. Roman centurions spent their holidays in Pompeii, Roman emperors chose the island of Capri, and no Victorian gentleman would have considered a Grand Tour of Europe without a stop-off in Sorrento or Naples.

While Tiberius might have had difficulty in recognising Rome or Rimini today, he would find parts of his former playground hardly changed at all. Modern development has found it hard to come to grips with such a rugged coastline. The only changes, viewed from the sea, would be that instead of chariots negotiating the bends of the famous Amalfi drive, today a continuous stream of cars snakes from one end of it to the other.

Further south in the Cilento, bordering Basilicata little Italian seaside resorts like Santa Maria di Castellabate haven't changed for 20 years and all around them are orchards full of cherries, pomegranates, peaches and figs. Campania is one of the most fertile regions of Italy and south of Salerno every acre, even the terraced hillsides, are covered with olive trees, lemon and orange groves. In early summer there are tiny artichokes and juicy white peaches the size of golf balls. Later on they are enormous. Buy plump long tomatoes to make your spaghetti sauces, orange-fleshed melons to serve with ham, watermelons to quench your thirst, blood red oranges, strawberries and apricots or dried figs flavoured with fennel.

The basic cooking of Campania involves imaginative use of a few basic ingredients: olive oil, fresh vegetables, pasta, seafood and cheese — particularly *mozzarella bufalina* from the buffaloes that graze on the flat plains below Naples. The people here don't eat much meat, except for the milk-fed veal from Vesuvius, but there are some meat dishes worth trying, like *bistecca alla pizzaiola* (steak with tomato, garlic and oregano), pot roasts with garlic, meatballs, *trippa alla napoletana*, and stews made with kid and rabbit.

There is plenty of seafood (swordfish, tuna, ray, octopus), although lobster, scampi and squid can be fairly expensive. Try *linguine* (pasta) with scampi or lobster if you can't afford a whole plateful. Cheaper are bass and bream, sardines, anchovies (eaten marinated with lemon and olive oil, vinegar, garlic and parsley) and shellfish of every variety. Shellfish are often put into soups *alla marinara* (with clams and mussels); there are giant prawns in garlic; vast plates of *fritto misto* gently fried in batter and mussels are served on the pizzas.

The Neapolitans claim to have invented many of Italy's most colourful and traditional dishes: pizza, spaghetti *al pomodoro, mozzarella in carrozza* among others. And there are more toppings for Neapolitan pizza than you can possibly imagine. Most combine *mozzarella* cheese with tomatoes, basil and oregano, with optional extras like anchovies, olives, *salame*, ham, capers ...

Pasta is mostly 'hollow'; *fusilli, linguine, cannelloni*, served simply with olive oil, tomato, garlic, basil and sometimes hot pepper. A spaghetti favourite is *alla caprese* with tuna fish, tomatoes and olives. They eat *lasagne* too and *gnocchi*. You'll find hearty soups made with beans, lentil and chard, tomatoes filled with rice, and lots of vegetable dishes using aubergines/eggplant and sweet peppers.

Cheeses are excellent. Try *mozzarella* sliced with tomatoes and olive oil, or fried (see p. 136). Other cheeses to try are the sharp *provole, provoloni, scamorze, trecce, caciocavalli, pecorino* and *ricotta*, which is made into a sweet turnover called *sfogliatelle.*

EMILIA ROMAGNA

Rimini, Riccione, Cattolica, Milano Marittima, Bologna and San Marino, Parma, Modena and Ferrara.

Emilia Romagna is between Lombardy and Tuscany. It is a rich agricultural area with its towns displaying much evidence of its Etruscan, Roman, Byzantine and Renaissance past. Bologna boasts Europe's first university; Dante was buried in Ravenna and Parma has a wonderful opera house.

Emilia Romagna has some of the best food in Italy. It is the home of 'bolognese' sauce, Parma ham, *mortadella* sausage, *tortellini*, Parmesan cheese and Lambrusco wine.

Of all the regions it is most proud of its 'home-cooking'. Pastas are home-made with eggs and there are endless varieties, many shaped into different kinds of parcel that are filled with meat, vegetables or cheese. They also eat a lot of *polenta* (a maize pudding) especially with game, creamy risottos and vegetable soups of which *minestrone* is the most famous.

Along with *mortadella* sausage (a load of old baloney!) from Bologna, the region produces all sorts of pork specialities and Italy's most famous ham, the *prosciutto* of Parma. You could also try: *zampone* from Modena (pig's trotter stuffed with pork and sausage) often eaten with lentils; *cotechino*, a fresh pork sausage slightly salted and spiced, usually served boiled; *coppa*, and umpteen salamis.

Along the beaches you'll see restaurants grilling anchovies or little squid on spits over wood coals, although some of the fish will be frozen. You might get sturgeon from the River Po and river trout and pike. At Ferrara eels are caught in traps, fattened and grilled fresh or roasted and then pickled in vinegar. vinegar.

If you happen to be up in the woods for a picnic you might see some truffle hunting taking place. There are excellent mushrooms too, but you have to know which ones are edible.

Since Emilia Romagna produces some of the best fruit in Europe you'll be spoilt for choice: orchards in summer will be bursting with cherries (the best are from Vignola), pears, apples, apricots, plums and peaches.

Italy's most famous cheese *parmigiano reggiano*, comes from Reggio Emilia, but other cheeses worth trying include *pecorino* from the mountains, *ricotta*, the soft *squaquarone*, *provolone piacentino*, the sharp *robiola* and the mild *soliole*.

Rich sweets and walnut and herb liqueurs end most meals in these parts.

FRUILI-VENEZIA GIULIA

Trieste, Udine, Aquileia, Lignano, Grado, Sistiana and Duino comprise this region, the area of Italy closest to Yugoslavia, with mountains, plains and good beaches.

Rustic home-cooking is what you'll find here in this northern region; open fires in the old fashioned kitchens and hams like the famous San Daniele hanging from the ceiling.

Cooking can be a little on the heavy, if hearty side. Flavours are strong (they use a lot of cumin and poppyseeds, horseradish and paprika) and there's a recognisable middle-European influence on some dishes.

There are many risotto dishes and *polenta* too, thick soups of beans, vegetables, barley, corn (try *bobici* made with fresh corn), fish chowders and *pasta e fagioli* a delicious soup made with beans, garlic and pasta.

Vegetables include asparagus, spinach, and *topinambur* (knobbly Jerusalem artichokes). *Radicchio rosso* and *radicchio verde* make salads more interesting and are also eaten grilled. Try *brovade* too, turnips cooked in the grape pressings left after the region's famous wines have been made and then grated into long shoelaces, sautéed or added to soups.

Spaghetti is hand rolled and eaten with fresh sardines; *ravioli* are filled with vegetables, brains, and herbs and served in a meat broth and *gnocchi* is sometimes stuffed with prunes or apricots.

Apart from the San Daniele ham, which some people rate even higher than Parma ham, look for small smoked *sauris, luganeghe, sopresse* and *musetto* (pork crackling) used in soups, *zampetti* (pig's feet) and *sanguinacci* (blood puddings).

They eat a lot of game, roasts with herbs, liver cooked in the oven, pork, goose, chicken, turkey and spicy meat balls similar to those in Yugoslavia.

Fish include lemon soles, clams, sardines, mussels, scallops, rays and golden coloured *dorades* and you can get fresh river trout inland.

Cheeses include smoked *ricotta, montasio* and *pecorino* which comes seasoned with anchovies. *Strucolo* is like a strudel but stuffed with onions and ricotta.

Pastries are often filled with dried or fresh fruit; *gubane* is a type of *Panettone*, filled with nuts and cider, raisins and rum.

Drink Tajut before lunch or dinner and follow it with a prune liqueur.

LATIUM (LAZIO)

Rome, Santa Severa, Sabuaudia, San Felice Circeo, Sperlonga, Terracina, Ronciglione and the Island of Ponza are all in Latium. The cooking of Latium (or Lazio) has been influenced a great deal by the regions that surround it and by other races, from the Etruscans to the Jewish community in Trastevere from whom tender artichokes cooked *alla Giudea* (fried crisply in olive oil) get their name.

To the ancient Romans, food was entertainment and at banquets it arrived elaborately dressed up — with salt or honey added to disguise the fact that it may well not have been at its freshest.

Romans eat a lot of everything: tripe and oxtail, baby spring lamb, *saltimbocca alla Romana, pecorino* cheese, vegetables and fruit. Most meals are washed down with Frascati, the wine from the hills.

Roman meals are generally substantial and hearty. Romans do not believe that you should have any room left for pudding when you've finished, although they do claim to have invented cheesecake, made with *ricotta* cheese.

Most meals begin with a big bowl of pasta: *all'amatriciana* (tomatoes, red peppers, garlic and bacon), *alla carbonara* (bacon, eggs and black pepper), or *all'aglio e olio* (olive oil and garlic). *Pecorino* cheese, which the region produces in large quantities, is often sprinkled on the top. If you don't have pasta you may be offered *gnocchi* (made with semolina), a bowl of soup made with chickpeas, pork rind and beans, or *stracciatella*, a clear soup into which egg and cheese have been beaten.

Vegetables are mixed with other produce: peas are served with ham (*piselli e proscuitto*), tomatoes are stuffed with rice and *suppli* are rice croquettes stuffed with mince and *mozzarella*. The *mozzarella* in these parts is often made from buffalo milk. Fennel, sweet peppers and aubergines/eggplant will be in the markets.

Salads have unfamiliar names; look out for *misticanza*, a salad of chicory, endive, cress, rocket and other wild leaves or *puntarelle*. Salads are usually dressed with olive oil and lemon; some are even fried with garlic (*strascinati*).

Of the meats, *saltimbocca alla Romana*, veal with ham and sage, is a popular dish all year round, while the tiny *abbacchio* (lambs) are eaten roasted with sage, garlic, rosemary and anchovy paste in springtime. Italians do not like older lamb, finding it much too fatty. *Fritto misto* is a dish made with brains, sweetbreads, artichokes and courgettes/zucchini; chicken is cooked *alla diavola* or *alla cacciatora*, and hearty dishes are made from oxtail with *alla vaccinara* appearing on most menus. You may find wild boar (*cinghiale*) in a sweet and sour sauce (*agrodolce*) and suckling pig roasted over a spit.

Fish are often cooked in casseroles with vegetables: squid with peas or artichokes, eels with peas. But fresh fish supplies may be limited. Fish costs more than meat.

Most meals end with fruit: yellow and white peaches, watermelons, Nemi strawberries and good grapes or *zuppa inglese*, which is supposed to have originated in these parts, Sambuca is the most famous liqueur.

LIGURIA

The Italian Riviera: Bordighera, Diano Marina, San Bartolomeo, Laigueglia, Alassio, Santa Margherita, Sestri Levante, Portofino, Santa Margherita, San Remo and Genoa.

Liguria's coastline stretches in an arc from the French border down to Tuscany. There are big built-up seaside resorts and small fishing villages where wealthy Italians have magnificent villas and moor their yachts offshore. Liguria has a great deal to offer in the way of food: some of the best olive oil in Italy, excellent herbs and vegetables from the terraces that drop down to the sea, and wonderful sauces like the Genoese *pesto*. Sadly the seas are becoming more and more over fished and polluted in northern Italy (Genoa is the largest port in the Mediterranean) and fresh fish can be expensive. In most of the seaside resorts you can buy from barrows that are wheeled through the towns in the early morning. *Gianchetti* are tiny fingernail sized fish — you boil them whole and serve them with olive oil, parsley and lemon.

If you happen to be in Liguria on the second Sunday in May, you should visit Camogli where tons of fish are fried in an enormous *padellone* (frying pan) five metres wide. In June there is a festival at Lavagna where the fish are baked on slabs of slate. Apart from the *buridda* (fish soup), molluscs are stewed or made into soups, risottos are flavoured with fish and *cappon magro* is an elaborate salad of mixed vegetables, fish and crustaceans, piled up into a pyramid and served with a rich garlic and anchovy sauce.

Almost everything in Liguria is flavoured with fresh herbs, and most of the dishes use vegetables cultivated in the mild climate: sage, basil, rosemary, parsley, celery, garlic, onions, fennel, artichokes, beans, mint, borage, thyme, marjoram and, of course, olives which go not only into the oil but into a *pane di polpe*, a flat bread filled with pitted olives and flavoured with white wine. The *focaccia*, a salted bread made with olive oil and sometimes cheese or olives, sage or onions originated in Genoa. They are eaten as snacks all over Italy and sold in *fornaio*.

One of the region's most famous dishes is *torta pasqualina*, a pie filled with spinach, artichokes and cheese, served in the old days to sailors returning from sea. *Fagioli e cipolle*, beans with onions, is a popular *antipasto*, and vegetables are often stuffed (*farciti*).

In the mountains there are walnuts, truffles, chestnuts, wild mushrooms, juniper berries and olive groves.

Sauces are almost all based on olive oil. The most famous is *pesto*, made with basil, garlic, *pecorino* and pine nuts, all pounded together with a pestle and mortar. It is served with pasta (*trenette*) and with *troffie*, little potato *gnocchi*. Other sauces include *maro* which uses fresh broad beans. There are sauces made with walnuts, artichokes, anchovies, pistacchios and oysters.

Meat is not widely eaten, although *cima Genovese* (cold veal stuffed with calf's brain, onions and herbs) is a speciality, and they eat roast rabbit.

As for sweets, try *biscotti del Lagaccio* made with fennel seeds, *pandolce*, an orange flavoured cake, baked peaches, candied violets and *chinotti* (bitter orange), as well as the famous *amaretti di Saronno* that you'll see sold in big red square boxes in *alimentari*.

LOMBARDY (LOMBARDIA)

The Lakes: Como, Iseo, and the western bank of Lake Garda, Milan, Bergamo, Brescia and Mantua are in this region.

Lombardy is an inland, largely agricultural region with a lot of dairy farming, dominated by Milan. Scenically it is very varied, from the fir covered alpine slopes and numerous rivers and lakes to the rice fields in the low flat Po River plain that produce the rice for the famous risottos. There is plenty of freshwater fish, the pork, poultry and beef is good, and the region is also known for its fruit, vegetables, cheeses (*Bel*

Paese, grana and *Gorgonzola*) and pastries. The cooking varies considerably from town to town.

Along the shores of the lakes and in the foothills of the Alps you can eat in little family-run country inns (*osterie*), while in the big cities like Milan there are some of the most sophisticated restaurants in Italy.

Perhaps the most famous Lombardy dish is *risotto alla Milanese*, cooked slowly in a small amount of stock which is coloured with saffron. Although Piedmont grows more rice than Lombardy, Lombardy uses it in more dishes, often as an alternative to pasta. Pasta is home made: *tortelli* are stuffed with spinach (or chard) and *ricotta*, or pumpkin, pickled fruit and cheese (*di zucca*). Or try *agnolini* stuffed with chicken, cheese and spices in chicken broth, or *ravioli* with butter and sage.

Minestrone is a Lombardy soup, thick with vegetables and beans, another soup to try is *alla pavese* a clear soup with poached egg, fried bread and cheese.

In Lombardy most meat dishes are boiled, braised or stewed for a long time. *Ossobuco* (shin of veal cooked in tomato) and *cotoletta alla Milanese* (a breaded veal cutlet) are the two most famous dishes. They eat hare in *salmi* (a rich wine sauce), *stracotto* (stews), goose stuffed with chestnuts, guinea hen baked in a clay oven, veal *tonnato*, boiled and served cold with a tuna sauce and *cazzoeula* (a mutton stew with ham, sausage, tomatoes and beans). Cold boiled meats are eaten with *mostarda di Cremona*, a pickle made with fruits, mustard, honey and white wine.

There are lots of Lombardy *salame* to try, like *felino* made with pork, white wine and garlic. *Busecca*, is a Milanese style tripe, *Bresaola* comes from a valley north of Milan, a cured filet of beef cut into thin slices and eaten with olive oil, lemon juice and black pepper.

As for freshwater fish, pike is served *alla comasca* (marinated and fried with an anchovy sauce), tench is stuffed *all'iseana* and you may see small flat water fish called *agoni* drying out in racks in the sun around Lake Como. They too are served marinated and fried with an anchovy sauce. *Corigone* are delicate white-fleshed fish like whiting. Pink trout are stuffed with herbs and baked and large lake sardines are grilled and served with fried *polenta*.

Cheeses include the hard *grana* and *bitto*, soft *mascarpone, Gorgonzola, crescenza*, freshly made *provolone, robiolini* and *taleggio* (best eaten soft and creamy) and sweet cheeses called *di tara*.

Milan's *Panettone* and Easter *Colomba* are eaten all over

Italy. Try also the *torta sbrisolona* from Mantua and Cremona's *torrone*.

PIEDMONT (PIEMONTE) AND AOSTA VALLEY (VALLE D'AOSTA)

Lake Maggiore, Lake Orta, Courmayeur, Cervinia, Aosta, Asti, Sestriere, Sauze d'Oulx, Claviere and Turin.

Piedmont, which includes the Lakes and their numerous resorts, is at the foot of the Aosta Valley over which tower Mont Blanc, Monte Rosa, Monte Cervino and a number of well-known ski resorts.

It has some of the highest mountains in Europe and one of the broadest plains in Italy through which the River Po meanders.

The wines are the best in Italy and Asti Spumante and Vermouth both come from the region. Piedmont cuisine is considered to be as good as any in Italy, a lot of the dishes are heirlooms! The cooking is basically mountain cooking, hearty and nourishing. They use a lot of high quality ingredients: butter, rice, white truffles, beef and game, asparagus and sweet biscuits among them, all considered to be the best of their kind in Italy.

Pasta is made by hand (they eat a lot of *lasagne*, and *gnocchi* made with potatoes). *Polenta* accompanies many dishes, especially poultry and game, and rice (the region produces three-quarters of the rice in Italy) is served as a risotto for a first course and is also used for sweets.

Sauces appear on everything, one of the best is *bagna cauda*, a 'hot bath' of olive oil, butter, garlic and anchovies into which you dip raw vegetables. *Fonduta* is also a dip, made with the local *fontina* cheese, milk and egg yolks. On the top are sprinkled one of the region's delicacies, white truffles, sniffed out by specially trained dogs in the south of Piedmont. Truffles are also stuffed into *agnolotti al tartufo* (large *tortellini*), and pheasants too are stuffed with them. Turin's famous *grissini* breadsticks are eaten with an *antipasti* of truffles, ham and butter.

Vegetables grow well at remarkable heights: sugar beet, lentils, wheat, edible thistles, wild mushrooms and varieties of lettuce. There are numerous cheeses, *tome, robiola, Gorgonzola*, and *castelmagno* among them.

Frogs are fried in butter or stewed in white wine. Meat dishes include *vitello valdostana*, veal chops stuffed with a soft cheese, and *lepre Piemontese*, hare cooked in Barbera wine and sprinkled with bitter chocolate. Chocolate appears too in *gianduia*, a cold chocolate pudding, and the famous chocolate pastry of Turin. There are excellent biscuits, and other desserts include *Monte Bianco* made with chestnuts, and *zabaglione*, whipped egg yolks with Marsala wine.

The Aosta Valley serves hearty food to suit the appetites of Alpine walkers. You'll find rich stews like the *carbonade* made with beer, soups made of chestnuts, rice and milk, and a *zuppa dell'asino* made with slices of black bread, soaked in red wine and sprinkled with sugar. There are trout from the mountain streams, sausages often preserved in terracotta jars and *boudins*, blood puddings.

SARDINIA (SARDEGNA)

Cagliari, Alghero, Santa Margherita di Pula, Capo Boi, Villa-simius, Santa Teresa Gallura, Santa Reparata, Baia Sardinia, Porto Rotondo, Porto Cervo, Porto Rafael, Olbia and Sassari.

Sardinia is a rugged attractive island just south of Corsica, still rich in tradition and local culture. It is almost as big as Sicily and is mainly agricultural and pastoral with mountains inland, most of the inhabitants living in cramped villages perched high on crags of rocks. There are pockets of tourism here and there particularly the Aga Khan's Costa Smeralda in the north-west which has several exclusive hotels and some attractive villas. There are some good beaches and a lot of rocky coves. It is the only region of Italy without a motorway!

Sardinian sheep, which outnumber the people, produce excellent *pecorino* and *ricotta* cheese which go to make a delicious pie (*sebada*) eaten as a dessert, onto which honey is poured. You can eat the wild boar that roam the mountains and steaks are served in a sweet and sour sauce. Suckling pig (*porceddu*) is roasted in the open air outside most small inland restaurants, along with *cordula* (lamb's guts), lamb and kid in season.

On special feast days gigantic roasts are prepared often with one animal inside the other! Sardinians also take a great deal of trouble over cooking game, deer, hares, rabbits and tiny birds, which are very popular. The birds are stuffed into bags of myrtle leaves and cooked slowly over an open wood fire to absorb the flavour.

Sausages are made with garlic, fennel or vinegar, and there are excellent hams and *salame*.

Wherever you go you'll notice a wide variety of bread; some are huge loaves, others in allegorical shapes (they grow a lot of durum wheat). One of the most popular, and now

available elsewhere in Italy, is the flat, brittle, *carta da musica*
— the shepherds' staple diet when out in the pastures. They
make it into a *pane frattau* (see p.137) as an *antipasti*.
Empanadas are made with pizza dough and stuffed with
cheese and vegetables, salami or fish, baked in the oven or
fried.

Vegetables are made into soups: *cavolata* consists of
cabbage, garlic and herbs in a broth, *favata* of broad beans,
pork and wild fennel, *fregula* of semolina with saffron and
cheese.

Along the coast *aragosta* or *astice* (lobsters) are the main
catch; there are plenty of mussels and clams; a *burrida* (fish
stew) is made with dogfish and skate. Look out for *cala-
maretti alla sarda* (stuffed baby squid), tuna and bream.

Sardinian honey has a strong flavour and is used in many
sweets. *Torrone* is locally made and there is plenty of fresh
fruit. *Suspirus* are small almond cakes flavoured with maraschino. The name means 'sigh'. They are sold wrapped in
paper, like sweets.

SICILY (SICILIA)

Cefalu, Palermo, Mondello, Taormina, Syracuse and the
Aeolian Islands (Lipari and Vulcano).

Sicily is the biggest island in the Mediterranean, about the
size of Wales. An island with an almost unfair share of history
(stone age tombs, Taormina's Graeco-Roman theatre, Greek
temples and Imperial Roman villas). Mt Etna smoulders
inland, motorways slice through olive and lemon groves and
through cornfields spiked with poppies; there are built up
towns and isolated fishing villages. The rugged coastline
around Taormina has coarse volcanic sand; at Cefalu in the
north the sands are golden; in the south they are almost
white. In the west the giant vats at Marsala brew the fine
dessert wine; the Aeolian islands to the north produce
tomatoes, capers and salt.

The food is a heritage of the numerous invaders who left
their mark on the island. The Normans contributed *stocca-
fisso* (salt cod); the Saracens sorbet, candied fruit and
marzipan, the famous *cassata* made with candied fruit; and
the Arabs introduced *trii* — strings of pasta.

Pasta is still made in Sicily, and the Sicilians are great
eaters of it. They regard soup as a poor 'northern' alternative
and have contributed many excellent sauces to the Italian
cuisine, many based on their outstanding fresh vegetables. In
Sicily the flavour of tomatoes is so good they hardly need

anything else with them. Citrus fruits are grown in larger quantities than any other part of Italy. You'll see almond and fig trees and, in the markets, excellent vegetables: giant aubergines/eggplant the size of rugger balls, plaits of garlic, red, green and yellow peppers.

There is very little meat, but fish is excellent: swordfish (*pesce spada*) is stuffed with brandy, mozzarella and herbs and grilled; pasta is served with fresh sardines; red mullet is grilled with orange peel and white wine (*triglie alla Siciliana*).

As for sweets, Sicily is worth visiting for the *cannoli* alone, fried pastries stuffed with *ricotta*, candied fruit and chocolate and every cake shop window is filled with *frutti di marturana* (realistic fruit made out of marzipan).

THE MARCHES (MARCHE)

This is the region of the central Adriatic: Gabicce, Pesaro, Senigallia, San Benedetto del Tronto, Arcevia, Urbino, Macerata, Ascoli Piceno and Ancona.

The Marches have fine sandy beaches, high cliffs along the Conero Riviera, mountains inland and low plains, Rossini was born at Pesaro, Raphael in Urbino and there are many art galleries to visit. The most famous wine is Verdicchio.

It is not a particularly gastronomic area and the cooking is influenced by the fact that The Marches are surrounded by five other regions not least of all by Emilia Romagna which means that you'll find plenty of stuffed pasta dishes and thick meaty sauces. The best-known pasta dish is *vincisgrassi*, sheets of pasta layered with cream, chicken livers, ham and truffles, named after an Austrian prince. But there are other pastas too and *ravioli* is often filled with fish.

As Ascoli Piceno is the fish capital of the Adriatic you'll find an enormous variety of fish. While a lot of them may well be the same as those you find in other regions, in typically Italian fashion they'll have different names.

Fish soup (*brodetti*) is made with tomato, white wine, onions, garlic and sometimes saffron; whole fish are roasted on spits. Cuttlefish are stewed with peas, or stuffed; sole is cooked in white wine; scampi is grilled; brochettes of *uccelli di mare* (small squid and cuttlefish) are breaded and browned with herbs; and there are molluscs too numerous to mention, cooked with herbs.

Meat is grilled on a spit but mostly it is cooked in a sauce (*in potacchio, alla cacciatora, in salmi*). Sometimes the sauces are of cheese and ham, flavoured with rosemary, wild fennel, or sage.

The *salame* is of a high quality, try the smoked *prosciutto* from Montefeltro, and the highly acclaimed *salame* from Fabriano.

Certainly there are a lot of good herbs and vegetables: celery, chard, asparagus, mountain mushrooms, cardoons and lots of olives, often stuffed with meat or herbs and then fried — one of the delicacies of Ascoli Piceno.

The best cheeses are the *caciotte* from Urbino and the mountain villages, the *pecorinos*, the soft *bazzoto*, and *ricotta* — used in fillings for cakes, on pizzas and in flat buns called *cresce, piadine* and *crostoli*.

TRENTINO ALTO ADIGE

Riva, Madonna di Campiglio, Canazei, Moena, Pozza di Fassa and San Martino di Castrozza, Solda, Merano, Selva di Val Gardena, Santa Cristina, Ortisei, Corvara, Bressanone, Brunico, Vipiteno, Trento and Bolzano.

These two regions are known primarily for their winter sports. The Alto Adige, bordering Austria, is entirely mountainous while Trentino has both summer and winter resorts and borders the Veneto and the top of Lake Garda.

The cooking is basically simple but often hearty. Mountain pastures produce some of the best butter in Europe, and excellent cheeses. Herbs, fruit and vegetables grow well and olives and lemons appear in some parts of Trentino.

In Trentino they eat *polenta* served with cheese, mushrooms, *salame* and eels. They are fond of *gnocchi* and pasta, stuffed chicken and partridge and pickled meat (*carne salada*).

In Alto Adige, the Austrian influence on cooking is marked, soups are often made with wine, and you may find *gnocchi* (*knoedel*) floating in them. Stews are hearty, and roast meats are often accompanied by sauerkraut, potatoes or apple fritters. Sauces may be made with horseradish.

The *salame* is excellent and includes *speck*, all sorts of sausages and *wuerstel*. Breads are made with wheat and rye. There are also numerous trout hatcheries and the fish are caught in the streams and lakes (of which there are over 600).

Sweets include *strudel*, and as well as fresh fruit, there are strawberries, blueberries and red currants many of which go to make the traditional sweets of the region.

TUSCANY (TOSCANA)

Viareggio, Forte dei Marmi, Marina di Massa, Punta Ala. Porto Ercole, Livorno, the island of Elba, inland spas like Montecatini, mountain resorts like Abetone, cities like Siena, Lucca, Pisa, and, of course, Florence.

Tuscany is roughly in the centre of Italy. Its scenery ranges from wide sandy beaches backed by busy seaside resorts to its inland hillside villages surrounded by olive groves and cypresses, where if you're lucky you'll be staying in a beautifully converted old farmhouse, decorated to a far higher standard than, for example, France's *gîtes*. This is Italy's most sought after area as far as self-catering is concerned and many wealthy Italians have their second homes here, within driving distance (a car is essential) from hill towns like Fiesole and San Gimignano, Siena and Lucca. Here you can visit the marble and leather factories, old olive presses, umpteen castles and, of course, Florence, a treasure trove of arts, and the centre of the Renaissance where you can see the works of some of Italy's most famous sons: Michelangelo, Dante, Giotto, Leonardo, Botticelli, Boccaccio and Petrarch among them.

Chianti is Tuscany's most famous wine but its food doesn't have quite as far reaching a reputation. It basically consists of good home-cooking using fresh local ingredients. Tuscan women are very possessive about their dishes and they wouldn't dream of serving up anything that wasn't regional. They have a great respect for the earth, and in recipes ingredients are used for their own merits without being masked by sauces and added flavourings. Olive oil is the basis for virtually every dish.

Tuscany is not particularly fertile, the terraced hillsides are difficult and expensive to cultivate. Their main produce is wheat, olive oil, wine, white beans, vegetables, herbs, lean beef and about 100 varieties of *pecorino* cheese, and all are used in cooking. They eat more bread than pasta although their *pappardelle alla lepre*, strips of pasta with a 'hot' hare sauce is worth trying.

Tuscan bread is made without salt and is used in several soups and salad dishes (see pp. 130 and 137). Even stale bread goes into a *ribollita di pane*, a broth made with green cabbage, bread and white cannellini beans. The dish is so popular that there are often queues outside a restaurant in Fiesole that specialises in it.

Unlike in many other parts of Italy beef is excellent. A *bistecca alla Fiorentina*, a tender T bone steak, is the regional speciality, cooked quickly on a grill over glowing embers. Individual steaks can weigh up to one and a half pounds. You can also get *arista*, pork loin with the rib attached which is cut into a single piece and roasted. A *stracotto* is a beef stew cooked for a long time in red wine. You should also try *crostini di fegatini* — tiny toasted squares of bread dipped in broth covered with a spread of liver pate (see. p. 134), sometimes capers and a little anchovy.

In the Tuscan hills there are plenty of pheasant, hare, birds, deer and occasionally wild boar to catch, all of which find their way into kitchens to be roasted, usually with a little wild rosemary. In those kitchens the Tuscan women use heavy earthenware pots for cooking and keep their precious olive oil in containers with a long spout. Olive oil from Lucca is considered to be the best in Italy; one dish to try it on in summer is fresh white beans, *fagioli all'olio*, served warm simply seasoned with olive oil, salt and pepper.

Pork is lean and wild boar from the Maremma region near Grosseto (*cinghiale di Maremma*), is also made into a *prosciutto* which you'll see hanging up along with spiced blood sausages.

Fish along the Tyrrhenian coast isn't as plentiful as it used to be but you should still be able to find *cacciucco alla Livornese* a fish stew made with chilli and tomato, served on toasted Tuscan bread rubbed with garlic and *baccalà alla Livornese*, salt cod cooked in tomatoes, black olives, garlic and sage.

As for sweets, Siena's *panforte* made with candied fruits is famous and there are numerous biscuits (*biscotti*) to dip into the *vin santo* dessert wine including *ricciarelli* made from honey and almonds. Try too a piece of *castagnaccio*, a cake made of chestnut flour and topped with pine nuts and raisins.

If you happen to be in Tuscany during the wine harvest go into the local *fornaio* and you will get a *schiacciata all'uva* — a tart made out of bread dough flavoured with aniseed or fennel seeds and filled with wine grapes. *Uva sotto spirito* are marinated in alcohol with water and sugar and kept for cold winter days.

UMBRIA

Assisi, Orvieto, Perugia, Spoleto, Gubbio and Norcia.

Umbria is a fairly isolated mountainous region in the centre of Italy, home of St Francis of Assisi, of Orvieto wines and the annual music, drama and dance festival of Two Worlds at Spoleto.

Umbria's cuisine is even more rustic than Tuscany's with simple use of wild herbs and meat roasted over burning wood. Sheep and goats graze beneath olive trees and pigs roam freely beneath oaks, feeding on acorns, sniffing out the famous black truffles of Norcia and Spoleto. They are so good that even the French import them. Umbria produces and eats more meat than any other region and pork is prepared in numerous ways one of which is to stuff a *porchetta*, a small pig, whole with herbs and wild fennel and then roast it. The hare and game, particularly wood pigeons from Norcia are especially prized and special pork butchers prepare a variety of *salame* and hams, fresh and dried sausages — even one with grapes.

In the mountain streams there are trout, pike, carp, eel and shrimp and they make a chowder called *tegamaccio*. Lake Trasimeno is one of the biggest freshwater lakes in Italy and the *larca* (a type of roach) caught in it is excellent.

There are plenty of vegetables, made into soups, pastas with sauces made with lamb or truffles, good cheeses and *bruschetta*, a bread made with olive oil and flavoured with garlic.

Of the sweets try *fichi girotti di Amelia*, dried figs filled with almonds and walnuts, and the *biscotti all'anice*.

VENETO

Lido di Jesolo, Bibione, Caorle, Sottomarina di Chioggia, Venice, the east bank of Lake Garda, (Peschiera, Bardolino, Garda, Macecine), Padua, Vicenza, Asolo, Verona, thermal resorts (Abano and Montegrotto) and winter sports resorts in the Dolomites (Cortina d'Ampezzo) are all part of this region.

The Veneto is an extremely varied region, it is the northeast part of the Po valley and includes mountain ranges, peaceful cypress-covered hillsides, flat plains full of blossoming pear, cherry and apple trees in springtime and the Adriatic coast with built up seaside resorts which have some of the best beaches in Italy. The hillsides around Conegliano produce sparkling white wines.

The most important commodity to the Venetians was salt from the lagoons around Venice and spices which the Venetians sold to European merchants at exhorbitant prices. When they ran out of spices they turned to sugar and then coffee. Venetian confectioners still have an excellent reputation for their sweets.

Salt is still used to cure fish, one speciality is *baccalà alla Vicentina*, salt cod simmered in milk served with *polenta*, a pudding made of maize flour that is also eaten with game and sausages. The region's best cheese, *Asiago* is also eaten with *polenta*. Rice forms the basis of *risi e bisi* (risotto with ham and peas). Risottos are also made with the black ink of squid, and chicken giblets, and rice is used in soups with fish, *salame*, meat or herbs. In Venice the soups may include tripe, bread or pasta.

Kid, hare, turkey, pigeon, goose (roast with celery in Padua and Treviso) and game are eaten extensively, often served with a spicy sauce called *peverada*, made out of giblets, anchovies and lemon cooked in oil. Another Venetian speciality is *fegato alla Veneziana* (calf's liver thinly sliced and cooked in butter with onions) and they are very fond of brains, heart and sweetbreads, as well as stewed lamb or veal lung (*fongadina*) and horsemeat!

Fish is varied, *coda di rospo* (monkfish tail) is grilled; red spider crab (*granseola*) boiled and served cold with oil and lemon. You can get huge scampi, shrimp, sea bass, sole and turbot. Most is fresh, and the fish market at Venice is a spectacle not to be missed. Inland the rivers produce eel, trout and freshwater shrimps.

The long leaved streaky red *radicchio* from Treviso is served as a salad with a little olive oil, or grilled. There are plenty of vegetables: tender celery, artichokes, beans, marrow from Chioggia, expensive *porcini* mushrooms that are sold dried in bags and some of the best asparagus in Italy — the white stemmed variety from Bassano del Grappa.

Many dishes combine sugar and spices: sultanas and pine kernels are added to rice puddings and doughnuts; sugar and cinnamon are added with butter to *gnocchi*; pine kernels and almonds are also made into *fave* (tiny macaroons). The Venetians eat a delicious biscuit called *le bisse* (see. p.166), and *zabaglione* is served ice-cold or whipped up with cream on cakes.

Look for small sweet figs (*segaligni*), the dark red cherries of Marostica and Verona's white and yellow peaches.

5

LOCAL MEAT AND MEAT PRODUCTS

MEAT

Italians are not great meat eaters. It is generally expensive and except for a few specific regions quality isn't particularly good. On the whole they eat more veal than beef. Here and there you'll get pork, young lamb, kid, wild boar, rabbit, hare and game.

An Italian butcher's shop is very different from an English one, particularly outside large towns. Meat is not usually hung, particularly in the south as butchers slaughter their own meat and then sell it a day later. If it is very hot you won't see meat lying around. There might be a few carcases strung up with lungs, liver and everything else hanging out of them and a selection of game birds in the window. There's also usually a large slab of veal on the marble counter, ready to slice into paper-thin escalopes.

You *can* ask an Italian butcher for the cut you want but since they are different to ours it's simpler to do as an Italian housewife does; she goes to the butcher with a specific dish in mind and trusts him to give her the best cut for it. Meat is sold by weight (i.e. half a kilo of rabbit or lamb) which usually means you get a bit of everything.

There are basically three cuts: *primo taglio* is the best and used for *bistecca* (steaks), *fettine* or escalopes, *secondo taglio* for cheaper cuts like stews (*spezzatino*) or *involtini*, *terzio taglio* for soups.

There is no shortage of offal: white honeycombed slabs of tripe, trays full of brains or sweetbreads, a calf's head to put into a stew and soft calves liver to make the Venetian dish *fegato aila Veneziana*. Italians eat parts of animals that we don't. If in doubt, stick to meat that looks familiar.

The simplest way to cook meat in Italy is to buy *scaloppine* of veal, beef or even pork, to grill or fry gently in olive oil, adding lemon juice or capers, anchovies, tomatoes, onions and black olives. If you want to attempt a casserole, ask for meat for *spezzatino* (stew). Most Italian recipes for meat use white wine rather than red and cooking time is often long.

Pork products are eaten more than meat itself, with smoked ham, particularly Parma, a lot cheaper than it is here. With a few slices of melon or a couple of figs it makes a simple and delicious start to any meal. Each region has its own *salame* and sausages, it's probably best not to know what goes into making them!

Beef (*manzo*)

The best beef in Italy comes from the white Val di Chiana cattle in Tuscany. It is in great demand for the famous Florentine T bone steaks *alla Fiorentina*. Outside Tuscany, steak can be of dubious quality. All sorts of cheaper cuts are sold as 'steak' many on the bone but don't expect them to be tender unless you ask for *filetto* (fillet) or *contra filetto* (entrecote or sirloin).

In the south you'll find very little beef, the cattle work the land and slaughtering produces tough and often tasteless meat that needs a good strong sauce of tomato and garlic to make it edible.

Of the best cuts, *primo taglio*, topside or top rump cut from the round (*fesa*) is the cut used for the thin slices of beef that are treated like *scaloppine* of veal. Ask for *fettine di manzo*.

Secondo taglio, are usually marinated with herbs and wine before they are pot roasted, stewed or casseroled in the oven. Ask for *manzo per spezzatino* (stewing). You can also use this cut to roll into *involtini* or to add a sauce like *pizzaiola*.

The *bollito misto* (boiled meats) of the northern regions of Piedmont, Lombardy and Emilia Romagna is a very tasty stew that combines beef with chicken, veal, calf's head and pork sausage. It is often served with a *salsa verde*.

In Rome they eat a rich oxtail stew called *coda alla vaccinara*. And in the Piedmont, *carpaccio*, are wafer thin slices of raw steak, marinated in oil and lemon. Try them with thin slices of Parmesan and raw mushrooms or with a little olive oil and black pepper.

Mince may not be on sale but once you've chosen your piece of meat the butcher will mince it for you.

Kid (*capretto*)

The best kid comes from Rome where the leg is used for casseroles and roasts. You can buy it almost all year round and it is sold by weight not by the cut. Baby ones weigh about 5-6 kg. Don't buy it if it is any bigger. In Sardinia look out for *corda*, strips of baby kid.

Lamb (*agnello*)

Italians rarely eat old lamb (*agnello*) (they hate fatty meat), but in springtime roast the tiny milk-fed lambs (about a month old). *Abbacchio alla cacciatora* is a speciality of Rome and the young lamb is cooked very slowly in a pot with sage, rosemary, garlic and anchovies.

If you do want a leg to roast (*cosciotto*), you will probably have to order it in advance and chops won't be ready cut you'll have to ask for them specifically. Try coating them in egg and breadcrumbs into which you've grated a little Parmesan.

Pork (*maiale*)

Pork is essentially a winter dish and you won't find much around during the summer. Cuts are different to ours. Italian butchers bone the leg and sell slices of it (*prosciutto di maiale*) for frying like veal escalopes. They use the loin for roasting (rolled and boned) and for chops. Roast pork (*arista*) is cooked on a spit. If you haven't got one you could braise the loin in milk (*maiale al latte*) as they do in Bologna, or attempt a *casoeula*, a Milanese pork stew. Roast suckling pig (*porceddu*) and wild boar (*cinghiale*) are both specialities of Sardinia, but you're unlikely to want to tackle either of them yourself.

Suckling pig

You're much more likely to eat your pork as smoked ham or in pate or *salame* (see 'Meat Products').

Poultry and Game

There are special shops that sell poultry called *polleria* or

37

pollame. The best chickens come from Tuscany — the leg-horn variety with yellow legs, they are eaten all over Italy and the Italians do much the same with them as we do. There's a tiny hen called a *mugellesi* from the same region that's never eaten because of its ability to sit on more eggs at one time than any other chicken. When they spread their feathers out their heads practically disappear into their bodies. Their tiny brown eggs are highly regarded but the hens don't much like giving them up.

In butcher's shops most of the chickens you'll see will be the yellow corn-fed ones, battery hens are sold in super-markets (*fattoria*). Whole chickens are *intero*. You can buy chickens cut up (*polite a pezzi*), *alette* or *ali* are wings, *coscia*, leg and chicken breast (*petto di pollo*) is used in a variety of dishes and made into galantine.

For stock or soup buy a *gallina da brodo* (older chicken, a half (*mezza*) will do. Or just a carcass (*pollo busto*). Capons are also used to flavour soups and give a richer taste.

For roasting, ask for a *pollo da fare al forno*, for casseroles a *pollo da fare spezzatino*.

Guinea fowl (*faraone*) are casseroled or roasted but to avoid them drying out in cooking they are usually wrapped in *prosciutto* or *pancetta* (steaky bacon) or cooked in a sauce. Squab has a strong flavour and is used in stuffings for pasta. And tiny birds *ucelletti* (rarer these days than they were) are roasted on spits or stuffed into bags of myrtle to absorb the flavour.

In the north game and small birds are often served on a bed of *polenta*, in the centre and south of Italy with pieces of fried bread.

Italians are very keen on game, although the quality isn't as good as ours. There usually isn't a specific hunting season, the birds are wild and shot at random. Moorhen, partridge, pheasant, quail and pigeon, are likely to be available most of the year, although you'll find more game around in winter. Game is usually cooked roasted on the spit or sometimes in casseroles. Pheasant is stuffed with fruit in Lombardy, and quail is cooked with white grapes in Tuscany.

Unless you're spending Christmas in Italy you probably won't be cooking a whole turkey, although the breast is used in a variety of dishes. In Bologna in autumn they use the precious truffles from Alba for *cotoletta di tacchino* — turkey breast with Parmesan, Parma ham and truffles.

Most large supermarkets that sell meat will have a good selection of game birds and poultry, whole and cut up into portions, ready cleaned.

Rabbit (*coniglio*) and Hare (*lepre*)

Rabbit is popular; it is mostly made into stews and sold cut up into pieces. Hare has a stronger flavour and is made into a stew with pine nuts and sultanas and served as a sauce to go with the thick strands of *papperdelle* pasta.

Veal (*vitello*)

Veal is the most popular meat in Italy. It is about the same price as here. The best veal is from milk fed calves less than three months old (*lattante*). The meat is nearly white, lean and exceptionally tender. Most of it is from Lombardy, and some from Vesuvius in southern Italy.

Vitellone is an older animal, about twelve months old which has been eating grass in the fields. Italians eat a lot of it in different forms, but it is really a young beef.

Scaloppine or *picatte* are the most popular cuts, they are cut very thin and flattened and take only minutes to cook. They are used for the *involtini* in the classic dish *saltimboca alla Romana* (see p. 162).

Osso buco is the braised shin or back leg shank and in the north it is as almost as popular as *scaloppine*. It is a speciality of Milan. The shins are sawn into pieces (see p. 159). In Trieste they cook the shin whole and carve it at the table. The marrow is taken out with a special fork; some people think it is the best bit. In Genoa they eat (*cima*) the breast of veal stuffed and pressed, served hot or cold.

Veal chops (*nodino di vitello*) are usually cut from the loin with the bone attached. Buy *fettine di vitello* for a flat escalope. Or to make a veal chop *alla Milanese* (in breadcrumbs) ask for a *costolla di vitello da fare alla Milanese*.

A lovely summer dish is cold roast veal with tuna (*vitello tonnato*), a speciality of Piedmont and Lombardy. The tuna is blended with capers, anchovy fillets, lemon juice and olive oil and spread over a flat plate of veal.

Venison (*cervo*)

Both venison and baby deer (*cappriolo*) are roasted and usually marinated first with juniper berries.

Offal (*frattaglie*)

Liver Calves' liver is the main ingredient for the Venetian dish *fegato alla Veneziana* (see p. 158). The liver is as soft as butter and is combined with onions. The butcher will slice it wafer thin. Pork liver (*fegato di maiale*) is sold wrapped in caul fat (*rete*) the membrane covering the intestines. Chicken livers (*fegatini di pollo*) are used for a number of dishes.

Calf's Head and Feet These are delicacies used in soups and stews.

Brains and Sweetbreads (cervella) These are also eaten, but they will probably need ordering in advance and are expensive.

Tripe This is the lining of the stomach and highly regarded. It has a chewy taste, looks like a large sheet of honeycomb and is sold on stalls in the street as a lunchtime snack. The tripe is pulled out of a bowl of broth and cut up on the spot for sandwiches.

There are two types, light and dark, both called *lampredotto* and butchers don't usually sell it partially cooked as they do here so it will be a greeny colour rather than white. It is often combined with garlic and potatoes.

In Florence they serve hot bowls of *lampredotto* in restaurants in winter; in Naples they eat it cold with oil and lemon juice but since the lighter variety absorbs sauces well it is often cut into strips and made up into a dish with vegetables.

Tongue (lingua fresca) Small calves' tongues weigh about a pound and a half (*lingua di vitello*). *Lingua di manzo* (beef) are bigger, about three pounds in weight, and are often put into a *bollito misto*.

MEAT PRODUCTS

There are hundreds of varieties of sausage and salami in Italy. Each region has its own speciality. The listing should help you identify the most popular — and possibly warn you off anything you don't want to try. Sometimes it's better *not* to know what goes into this kind of thing.

Bresaola

This is air dried beef, worth looking for but very expensive, even more so than Parma ham. It is made from the dry salted muscles from a leg of beef and is sliced very thinly. Usually rectangular and a deep red colour, the slices are eaten with a little oil and black pepper, or with fruit.

Carpaccio

This is raw best quality topside or fillet of beef, sliced transparently thin. Serve with a vinaigrette dressing or just lemon juice and olive oil.

Coppa

Coppa or neck of pork is a trade name for flattened pork meat — a sausage that looks more like a round, dark Parma ham. It is one of the most expensive salamis.

Cotechino

This pork sausage from Emilia Romagna is very popular. Eat it fresh (or salted for just a few days), seasoned with nutmeg and cloves. Italians boil it for about an hour (to take out some of the fat) and eat it with *bollito misto* (meat stew) or with lentils.

Luganega

This consists of mild pork sausage, coiled into a rope; it is good for cooking in recipes that call for pork sausage.

Mortadella

This Bologna sausage is the best-known cooked sausage in Italy. It can be of gigantic proportions (they hold competitions to see how big they can make them). It is pink, dotted with cubes of hard pork fat and sometimes pistachio nuts. There are dozens of varieties, the best being from Bologna. In the old days *mortadella* was made with minced pork, beef and/or horsemeat and pigs's stomach, encased in a shiny piece of gut. These days it is more innocuous and wrapped in plastic.

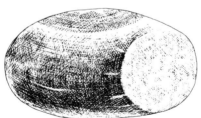

Mortadella

Pancetta

This salted streaky bacon is spiced and rolled up like a piece of salami. It can be eaten raw in sandwiches. In recipes it is used cut up into cubes or sliced thinly.

Parma Ham

This is the most famous and undoubtedly the best cured ham in the world. It is made from legs of fattened pigs in northern regions and salted with sea salt, washed, dried in the air and seasoned.

It has a sweet, delicate flavour and is sliced thinly and eaten with bread, or on a plate with melon, figs, or even peaches or kiwi fruit. Some say that the best comes from Parma, supposedly because the air of the hills from September to March when the hams are cured is superior to other regions. They also claim that there the pigs are given a better diet (the whey from Parmesan cheese), but there are lots of schools of thought about the best Parma hams.

The production of Parma ham is taken very seriously. I was lucky enough to stumble across the Casa del Parmigiano in Marostica (Veneto) near Vicenza, where the owner Gino Gastalbello told me how he came to be an expert *puntalore*, or ham sniffer. His 'nose' for hams won him first prize in the Veneto and third in all of Italy in a competition that takes place each October. These experts can tell whether the pig has been reared on fishmeal or acorns by sticking a bone 'needle' from a horse's ankle into a ham, and then sniffing it.

Parma ham

Certainly the ham he sold me was as soft as butter (which, incidentally should be eaten with it), not too salty and much better than the Parma ham we get in delis or restaurants here. It *is* expensive, but a little goes a long way. Avoid buying a piece and trying to slice it yourself.

Prosciutto (crudo)

This is the general name for all salted and air-cured hams

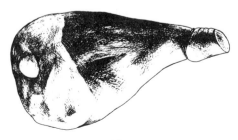

Prosciutto

42

that are eaten raw. It is used to wrap round and flavour game or small birds, on veal fried with mozzarella cheese, or on its own, sliced not too thinly as an *antipasto* with figs or melon. *Prosciutto di montagna* can come from virtually anywhere and may or may not be as good as Parma ham. San Danielle ham (from north of Udine) can be even better than Parma ham and even more expensive. *Prosciutto* (*cotto*), cooked ham, is eaten but it can be a bit tasteless.

Salame

There are hundreds of shapes and sizes of salami. The best will be types you *haven't* seen in supermarkets here. If you hesitate and don't seem to know what you're buying, the shop or market stallowner will probably let you have a bit to taste before you decide. Most are seasoned with salt and spices: pepper and garlic more often in the north and hot peppers, tomatoes and fennel seeds in the south. The Felino *salame* from Parma is even more expensive than Parma ham.

Zampone

From Modena, this is a sausage stuffed into a pig's trotter. It has a creamy texture and is highly regarded.

6
LOCAL FISH
AND SEAFOOD

FISH

Italians eat much more fish than they do meat, and it is usually cheaper. Wherever you are in Italy you won't be far from the coast, a lake or a river. Inland the rivers and lakes are teeming with tench and pike, trout, eels and shrimp. Along the coast, particularly in the south, you'll get squid and prawns, bream, brill, mussels, oysters, huge black swordfish and thick-fleshed tuna. However, pollution and over fishing have taken their toll of fresh fish in certain parts of northern Italy, particularly along the west coast around Genoa.

Italians don't mess about with their fish. They get up early in the morning and buy it almost before it has caught its last breath, either in the markets or straight off the early morning boats. Usually they cook it simply: baked without liquid in the oven, fried in a light batter or olive oil, or grilled either as steaks or as a whole fish, scored and brushed with oil.

Often they don't even bother to remove the head or even gut it. They are fond of stuffing fishes like bream and brill and baking them in the oven, and of chopping up bigger fish like tuna and swordfish into thick steaks which they simply put under the grill.

In several regions they throw a variety of fish (and their heads) into fish stews (like the Genoese *burrida*) and prepare fish soups (like the Sardinian *ziminu*). They don't usually bother with elaborate sauces, except in the south where they're not averse to adding a few tomatoes and anchovies, capers or onions.

Every restaurant along the coast in summer will serve bowls of steaming mussels, vast platters of *fritto misto* (mixed fried fish), rings of fried squid (*calamari*) and lightly fried prawns.

45

Identifying different fish by their Italian names is almost impossible as each region has its own, and often different, name for the same fish! Not only that, there are literally hundreds of varieties, any of which might turn up in the early morning catch. You'll probably get the best choice if you are holidaying along the Adriatic around Venice (don't miss the fish market there) and in Sicily.

If you are in an inland region Italian supermarkets do a good line in frozen fish. You can get *zuppa di pesce* (fish soup), *vongole* (clams) for spaghetti, even *fritto misto*. And if the children can't do without their fish fingers (*bastoncini*), supermarkets stock those too.

The best place to shop is the market. If there is one it will be down by the port. If not, get up early and find out where the fishing boats come in. Most holiday resorts will have a fishshop. You may also find that there's a van that will call at your villa or apartment on certain days of the week. Ask locally.

When buying, the eyes should be bright and protruding. They should not be dull and sunken into the flesh. The gills should be moist and red, not grey and if you prod the fish with your finger it shouldn't leave a dent in the skin.

The glossary below should help you identify some of the fish that appear on market stalls and give you an idea of what an Italian does with it.

Anchovies (*alici, acciughe, acciuga*)

Most anchovies are immediately tinned or put into brine but they are delicious grilled fresh. The fish have blue backs and silver sides and are caught at the time of the waning moon. Cook like fresh sardines.

Angler or monkfish (*rana pescatrice*)

This is a hideously ugly fish that swims in deep water close to the sandy bottom, with a huge mouth, and long filaments that wave around above it. Little wonder that they usually remove the head before they display it in the market (although it is used in soups). The tail known as *coda di rospo* is very popular in restaurants along the Adriatic. It is a thick-fleshed fish that's almost as good as lobster and is best simply split open and grilled or fried up like scampi (which it is often passed up as).

Bream (*dentice, orata, pagro, sarago*)

There are several varieties, lots of names. One has a gold spot on each cheek, another has thin yellow lines. It is a white-fleshed fish often baked and stuffed, or grilled with anchovy butter. *Dentice* are usually pink.

Brill (*rombo liscio*)

This is a flat fish of varying colours, similar to turbot but with a more delicate flavour. It is often baked.

Eel (*anguilla*)

The centre of the eel fishing industry is at Comacchio on the east coast although there are good eels along the west coast too. They are often sliced and threaded onto skewers and cooked over a spit or stewed in white wine. They were revered by the Romans who kept them as pets in special pools and fed them to the slaves.

Eel

Grey Mullet (*cefalo, muggine, dorato*)

This fish has numerous names and appearances. Wash it well, grill, bake, or poach and serve hot or cold.

Grouper (*cernia*)

Grouper is a plump oval fish, red or yellowish brown with dark patches. It has few bones, a delicate flavour and firm flesh. It tastes good baked and served cold. Stuff it with prawns and dried mushrooms or casserole with white wine.

John Dory (*pesce san pietro*)

This is a fairly expensive fish with a large head. It was named by St Peter who caught it and threw it back into the water after it made distressed noises, causing a dark spot to appear on each of its sides. It is common along the Adriatic and served in Venetian restaurants as *pesce bolito con maionnese*. It is a good fish for boiling as it has a good flavour and the firm white flesh fillets well. In Sicily it is known as *pesce gallo* and is cooked in Marsala wine. The head and bones make a good stock.

Ray, Skate (*razza*)

There are numerous varieties and the big ones sting. The thornback ray is like skate and the wings are eaten with black butter (*razza chiodata*), the guitar fish (*pesce violino*) is shaped like one and swims around Sicily. Don't be put off by the smell of ammonia when you buy it, it will disappear with cooking.

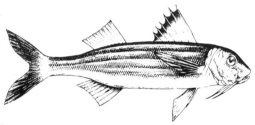

Red mullet

Red Mullet (*triglie*)

This fish is usually red with a delicate flavour and a lot of small bones. It is eaten grilled whole. Ask the fishmonger to scale it. Red mullet is often poached in white wine and tomato. In the Marche, it is baked wrapped in Parma ham and breadcrumbs.

Sardines (*sarde*)

Sardines are the most common fish of southern Italy, the smaller ones have the best taste. Grill or bake. Along the Adriatic they turn up as little sprats (*papaline*) that are fried like whitebait.

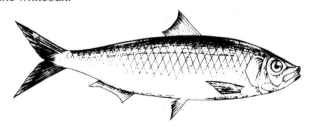

Sardine

Salt Cod (*baccalà*)

This appears as stiff planks of whitened fish sold in *aliment-ari*. They need soaking for at least 12 hours. It is eaten on Fridays and fastdays, particularly around Venice and the Veneto where they serve it with *polenta* stewed with anchovies, garlic and raisins. It is also fried with garlic and tomatoes, baked with tomatoes and herbs and in Naples fried with garlic, olives, capers and tomatoes.

Sea Bass (*spigola*)

Sea bass is silver with a dark back and white belly, a white firm-fleshed fish. Along the Adriatic they call it *branzino*. Big ones are cooked in a *court bouillon*, braised in white wine or baked stuffed with garlic and herbs.

Sea bass

Sole (*sogliola*)

This common fish is eaten grilled or fried whole. There are lots of different names: *lengua, palaia, sfoglia, lingua* among them.

Swordfish (*pesce spada*)

This is a very dramatic looking big fish with a shiny black body and long pointed snout. They are very common in southern Italy where they swarm past Sicily in early summer. The flesh is cut into thick chunky steaks and is a red steaky colour before it is cooked. They simply need grilling (see p. 154) for a few minutes as overcooking dries them out. On the island of Lipari, north of Sicily, at Filipinos (one of the best restaurants in southern Italy) they serve *bocconcini di pesce spada alla carbonella* — thin rolls of *spada* on a skewer stuffed with pine kernels, capers and olives.

Swordfish

Trout (*trota*)

Trout is fished in the northern lakes and rivers, the pink ones are from Lake Garda. In Lombardy they cook it in a sweet and sour sauce; in Umbria with black truffles.

Tuna, Tunny (*tonno*)

Blue fin tunny are caught in traps off Sicily and are one of the most common fish in the south from May to August, although there is a smaller variety found along the Adriatic. The best cut is the *ventresca* from the belly — a thick wedge of pale pink meat. It is best grilled, brushed with a little olive oil, or braised with white wine. If you buy it canned, look for *ventresca* on the label. It is served with cold veal, with mayonnaise and in salads.

SHELLFISH AND MOLLUSCS

Clams (*vongole, arselle*)

These small shellfish are served in trattoria all along the coast, *alla marinara*. Soak for an hour in slightly salted water, drain, put a little water in a saucepan, add the clams and put the lid on and cook over a high heat until all the clams have opened (about ten minutes). Then add garlic and parsley. Discard any that are still shut. The clams can be added to a tomato sauce and served with spaghetti. Small clams are called *arselle* in some regions.

Crab (*granceole, granchio*)

There are many varieties of crab. The big red spider crabs you get along the Adriatic are usually boiled, the meat is scooped out, seasoned with oil and mayonnaise and then put back into the shell. Along the Venetian lagoon, green, soft shell crabs are fried in batter and eaten whole. You'll see them in the markets in early May when they are changing

Crab

their shells and float to the surface and straight into the fishermen's nets.

Crawfish, spiny lobster (*aragostine, arigusta, astice*)

The best are from Sardinia (which has the same name for one of its wines). In Sicily they cook them in oil, with white wine, parsley and lemon. They can be boiled for about half an hour, split open and served hot with melted butter or cold with mayonnaise. You can also buy them cooked, ready to eat, if you can't bear to hear them squeal.

Cuttlefish (*seppie*)

Cuttlefish are oval shaped (up to 25 cm long) with eight short and two long tentacles. More tender than octopus, the tentacles are cut into strips and then fried into rings, they are stewed or boiled in their own ink, stuffed, or cut up and eaten cold in salads (the same can be done with squid — *calamari*). The fish secrete ink into little sacs which are used in Sicily in a *riso nero* (black rice) dish; in a stew served with *polenta* in Venice and with spinach in Tuscany. Before cooking you need to remove the guts, eyes and beak. The smaller ones are best. Tiny, tiny ones can be eaten whole, fried. Some fishmongers may clean the larger ones for you.

Cuttlefish

Date Shell (*dattero di mare*)

This is slimmer than a mussel and brown. It is found along western coasts, and often made into a soup.

Mantis Shrimp (*cannocchia*)

This is a delicately flavoured crustacean like a pale flat prawn, widely found in Emilia Romagna and around Venice. Its front legs are extensions of its mouth. It is usually served plain in its half shell, with oil and lemon (simmer in water for 10 minutes) or, when cooked, peel and fry in flour, egg, wine and olive oil.

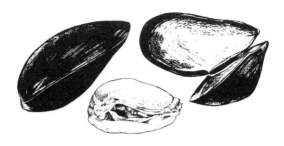

Mussels

Mussels (*cozze*)

Eat raw with lemon juice, or cook as a soup with tomatoes, vegetables, white wine and olive oil, or simply fry in olive oil, garlic and parsley until all are opened.

Octopus (*polipi, polpo, polpetielli*)

This fish is much tougher than squid or cuttlefish and needs stewing slowly. You can see the fishermen bashing them on the quayside and flattening them with a wooden paddle. The eyes, beak and internal parts should be removed. The best have a double row of suckers.

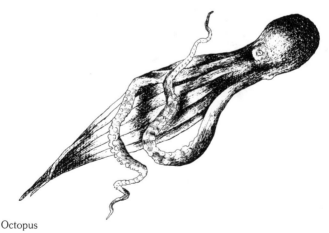

Octopus

Oysters (*ostriche*)

They are available in months with an 'r' in them. Eat raw with lemon (risky), you can open the shells with a sharp knife. Throw away any that are not tightly shut or that float in water.

Oysters

Prawns (*gamber(ell)i*) and Shrimps (*gamberetti*)

Prawns and shrimps are very similar. They are often sold uncooked in markets. Grill unpeeled, painted with olive oil and lemon juice or cook to serve cold with salads or mayonnaise. Tiny shrimps can be fried and eaten whole without peeling.

Scallops (*canestrelli*)

The scallop is a large-shelled mollusc, the edible part is the white muscle. You can buy them ready opened. They need soaking in salted water for half an hour. Sauté in a little wine, parsley and garlic, or boil until the flesh is firm. Use their shells as a dish.

Scampi/Dublin Bay Prawn

These are bigger than prawns or shrimps, grey or pink and most common along the Adriatic. Tails are often boiled and served with melted butter.

Sea Urchins (*ricci di mare*)

These prickly-spined round creatures cling to the rocks and give bare-footed swimmers a nasty fright. They are difficult to pick without gloves. They are sold cut in half so that the red roes can be scooped out, eaten immediately if you fancy taking the risk, raw with lemon juice.

Squid (*calamari* or *calamaretti*)

Squid is like an octopus but with two extra tentacles. It is

Squid

found most commonly in the north around Genoa and along the Adriatic. Cook like cuttlefish, cut up and dredge with flour and fry in rings, or simmer stuffed with its own tentacles in a sauce of tomatoes and oregano. To clean, cut off the end of the head with the tentacles and pull away the rest from the body, clean out the insides under running water.

7

LOCAL FRUIT AND VEGETABLES

FRUIT

Fruit has always been important to Italians; it was the Romans' staple food. Apples were their favourite fruit, apricots and peaches were imported and therefore expensive, dates came from Africa, melons the size of oranges came originally from Persia, while cherries and figs were home-grown.

Fresh fruit ends most meals in Italy, at home and in restaurants where, a huge basket of fruit will be on display, overflowing with strawberries, juicy white-fleshed peaches, succulent figs or perfect Muscat grapes. Somehow in Italy fruit seems to be of better quality than any that makes its way onto fruit stalls here.

Italians combine their fruit with other things: figs or melon are eaten sliced as an *antipasto* with thin slices of Parma ham, figs are eaten with fennel seeds, pears are stuffed with *Gorgonzola* cheese, peaches float whole in a glass of Asti Spumante, melon or strawberries are puréed with milk to make a refreshing summertime *frullato*, plums are stuffed into *gnocchi* and of course every conceivable fruit is made into ice cream. And when the summertime is over fruits of every description are preserved in bottles with spirits or liqueurs. Take them home and cheer up ice-cream or flan cases.

Wherever you travel in Italy you'll see fruit growing or freshly picked and for sale by the roadside: giant green water-melons ready to quench a summer thirst, orange skinned persimmon weighing down branches on an autumn day, cherries in early summer, pomegranates, lemon groves, oranges, plums, apricots, prickly pears on the cacti.

In country areas you can buy cheaply directly from the farmer or co-operative (as you can wine and olive oil). But you will have to buy a whole tray of fruit rather than just a kilo.

The following is a selection of fruits you might find in the markets and some ideas of what to do with them. The further south you go the earlier the season begins. Names often vary from region to region.

Apricots (*albicocche*)

Italian apricots are big and sweet, cheap and in the markets from June to July. They have much more flavour than apricots sold here.

Apricots

Cherries (*ciliege*)

Cherries come from Emiglia Romagna, the Veneto, Apulia and Campania (Sorrento). They are at their best in May, June and July, there are lots of varieties including white ones (*ciliege regina*). If you happen to be in the Veneto on the last Sunday in May don't miss the festival at Marostica where the locals eat cherries all day until the streets are so full of pips it's like walking on a pebbly beach. Cherries are bottled and used for sauces (on venison) and to make the liqueur Marachino. Italians pickle big cherries at home and in winter treat themselves to a couple to offset the cold. Look out for Borri chocolates filled with single cherries, sold in boxes or individually in cake shops.

Figs (*fichi*)

At the end of June and again in autumn the swollen purple or green fruit almost weigh down the branches of the fig trees. The juicy red flesh combines well with Parma ham as

Figs

an *antipasto*. Wash carefully as they tear easily, and peel off the outer skin. In Campania they are dried in the sun and seasoned with fennel seeds and bay leaves (*sproccolati*). You can often buy them very cheaply in trays.

Grapes (*uva*)

The best from Apulia and Sicily, are in the markets from July until November. They are much cheaper and of better quality than here. Don't miss the Moscata grapes, golden coloured and very sweet or the large, crisp *uva regina*.

Lemons (*limoni*)

Sicily produces the most lemons, you can see them on the trees almost all year round. Lemon trees are not just restricted to formal fields, your villa may have a tree in its garden. Use the peel in meat and fish dishes and squeeze the fruit to make a refreshing lemonade.

Loquats (*nespole*)

The loquat is a funny looking spring fruit the size of a plum. They are best when the yellowy coloured skin looks damaged or bruised. They are sometimes confused with medlars. Inside there are three shiny brown stones.

Melons (*meloni*)

Watermelons and a variety of cantaloupe are what you see most of in summer. The sweetest cantaloupes are from Modena. Any melon (apart from watermelon) can be served with thin slices of Parma ham as an *antipasto*. A good melon should be heavy for its size and have a sweet smell. The stalk

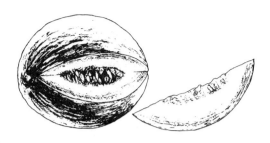

Melon

end should respond to gentle prodding. Look out for the small Charentais melons, round with a green skin and orange flesh.

Nectarines (*pesche noce*)

The nectarine is a smooth skinned variety of peach, reddish in colour with yellow juicy flesh. Handle carefully as it bruises easily. They are available all summer.

Oranges (*arance*)

Most oranges come from southern Italy, Sicily and Calabria. There are lots of varieties including small juicy blood oranges (*moro, tarocco* or *sanguinello*). The peel is often used candied in cakes and sweets.

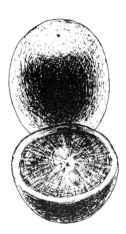

Oranges

Peaches (*pesche*)

A summer treat — Italian peaches can be as big as grapefruit and you can get the delicious white-fleshed variety too. They are sold by the roadside, in markets, or greengrocers' shops, or you can buy trays from farms. The largest quantity come from Campania and Emilia Romagna, and are in the shops from May or June until September.

Pears (*pere*)

Most come from the north and Emilia Romagna. They are more common than apples in markets, and there are lots of varieties. They are eaten a lot with cheeses like a *pecorino* and stuffed with *Gorgonzola* (see p. 167).

Persimmons (*cacchi, kaki*)

A winter fruit (October and November) that looks like a shiny orange tomato. The flesh is soft and juicy. If you pull the large stem off the top it leaves a hole big enough to put a spoon in. Eat only when fully ripe.

Plums (*susine*)

Plums are in the markets from June until August, most from Emilia Romagna and Campania. There are lots of varieties including Santa Rosa and a golden variety from Sicily.

Pomegranates (*melagrani*)

These are round fruit with a hard, red and yellow skin, originally from Persia. The seeds are used to make grenadine. Slice, pick out the red seeds from the bitter yellow membrane.

Pomegranates

Prickly Pears (*fichi d'India*)

Prickly pear is a cactus fruit covered in little sharp prickles. It is in the markets in late summer until early winter. It is long with a greenish orange skin and delicate pinky orange flesh. Eat chilled slices with a squeeze of lemon or lime, or with ricotta cheese. Be careful when you tackle it. Spear with a

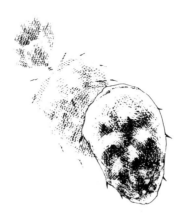

Prickly pears

fork and top and tail, then split lengthways and ease skin away from the flesh with the blade of a knife.

Strawberries (*fragole*)

An early summer fruit, some of the varieties are tiny like the *fragole dei boschi* (wild wood strawberries) which are grainy with an intense flavour. If you're lucky you can pick them yourself. Serve chilled, cut up in glasses with a little wine, liqueur, or fresh orange juice.

Watermelons (*cocomero, anguria*)

The best way of quenching a summer thirst is to sink your face into a wedge of watermelon. They are large, usually round, with dark green skin, bright red flesh and black pips. You can usually buy them by the roadside ready sliced, or by the kilo — some are enormous. If you happen to be in Florence on the Feast of San Lorenzo (patron saint of cooks) on 10 August you'll see thousands of them piled high on stands. Keep in the fridge covered in film and do not buy wedges that look woolly.

VEGETABLES

Italians today treat their vegetables with a great deal of respect. The Roman legions as they conquered fresh territories helped themselves to vast chunks of land and cultivated them. Cabbage became one of the most popular vegetables with the rich, while poorer people ate greens, nettles and broad beans.

Italians do a lot more with vegetables than we do; boiling, braising, grilling, sautéeing, baking, frying in batter, adding sauces, eating stalks, stems and even flowers, and generally turning what we might consider to be something rather boring into a delicious dish that stands on its own rather than just accompanying another part of the meal.

If you want to see a serious cook at work, just get up early and watch an Italian housewife choosing her vegetables from the market. You won't see her with a shopping list, she just picks out what looks particularly good and fresh that morning. Only when she gets home will she start thinking about how to cook it.

And there's no wastage; leaves of roots like radishes are pulled off and boiled and put into salads or stuffed into ravioli, and any other discarded part like the ends of asparagus or outer leaves of cabbage are put into soups or simmered down for sauces.

Artichokes (*carciofi*)

Artichokes are thistle like flowers that grow almost as weeds. They were first cultivated in the fifteenth century and considered an aphrodisiac at the time of the Renaissance. Italians do an enormous amount with their artichokes which come into season in winter and early spring and sometimes last the summer. The little ones have tender leaves and hardly any choke, they are usually eaten sliced and fried in olive oil in the traditional Easter dish of Rome, *carciofi alla Giudea*. In the north and centre of Italy the young artichokes are purple with long spikey leaves. You don't usually see them outside Italy.

The mammola artichokes are the big green globe-shaped ones and are grown in the south. If you've never eaten one before they can look rather unapproachable but they are well worth tackling.

Artichoke

When you buy artichokes choose globes with tightly closed leaves, if you're not going to cook them straight away you can keep them fresh by putting the whole thing, stalk first in water.

To prepare, wash well and leave to soak in water and vinegar or lemon for a while, cut away the outer green leaves, and trim the upper part of the rest of the leaves. Squeeze lemon juice onto the cut parts to prevent discolouring. Scrape out the hairy choke and boil head down in salted water until the bottom is soft to the point of a small knife. Eat by pulling a leaf off and scraping the flesh away with your lower teeth.

Serve with melted butter, hollandaise, or with vinaigrette, hot or cold. When you've eaten the leaves, the heart is tender and delicious. You can buy them in bottles *sott'olio* marinated in olive oil, lemon juice and wine.

Asparagus (*asparagi*)

Asparagus are in the markets from about February to April. There are many varieties; the most well known are the purple ones from Genoa. The best are the wild asparagus that grow around Rome, the asparagus from Ravenna and the thick white stems from Bassano in the Veneto. Close to the Swiss border they are thin and green, while the biggest (but least flavourful) are from Tuscany.

When they are very young all you have to do is boil them for a few minutes and serve with melted butter and freshly grated Parmesan. In markets, look for tips that are tight, pointed and firmly closed. Older asparagus need boiling for rather longer. Asparagus with less flavour can be baked in the oven (see p. 145).

Asparagus

Aubergine (*melanzane*)

Aubergine or eggplant are eaten a great deal in southern Italy where they are fried, baked or cut up in sauce for spaghetti. They were introduced into Italy from the Middle East at the end of the fourteenth century. There are several varieties, big and small: mauve glossy vegetables, or light purple with white patches and a thinner skin. Skins should be smooth, firm and unblemished. See p. 147 for *melanzane alla parmigiana*.

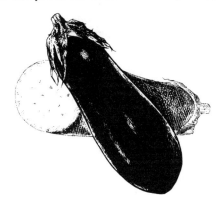

Aubergines

Beetroot (*barbabietole*)

Italians fry their beetroot coated in batter in hot oil and use the leaves and stems boiled for stuffing ravioli, in soups and cut up in salads. They also bake them whole with cream and Parmesan.

Broad Beans (*fave*)

The beans in their long knobbly pods are best when they are tiny and young, from April until the end of June, (the pods

Broad beans

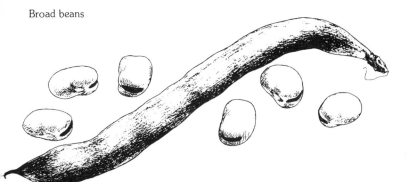

will be no more than four inches long). Peel off the outer layer of skin or it will turn black, and boil for a few minutes until the skins begin to pucker. Or eat them raw as an *antipasto* with ham. By summer overgrown beans can be tough. Try cooking them with enough water to cover, a little olive oil and chopped up tomatoes. The beans stay solid while the water evaporates.

Broccoli (*broccoli*)

Developed in Italy in Calabria from *brocco* meaning sprout, they have purple, white or green heads. Do not buy when flowering.

Cabbage (*cavolo*)

Cabbage is chopped up in soups, or eaten with pork and sausages. *Cavolo nero*, with no head is less strong and grown in Tuscany.

Cardoons (*cardi*)

These are the top stalks of thistle artichokes, grown in Umbria. Cook them in batter and fry in egg and breadcrumbs. They need peeling first and putting in water to keep them white.

Cardoons

Celery (*sedano*)

Celery is eaten fried, braised or boiled. It is used in sauces, and forms the basis of most vegetable soups, when the leaves are cooked as well.

Chard (*biete, bietole*)

Chard is a leafy vegetable with a long leaf a bit like spinach. It is used in soups; to stuff ravioli and fried in *frittata* and in salads. The thick white rib is eaten boiled like asparagus.

Chicory (*cicoria*)

Chicory is used in salads but also braised.

Courgette (*zucchini*)

Choose small, narrow ones, bright and glossy, firm not flabby for frying or to cut up for spaghetti sauces. In spring and early summer you can sometimes buy fresh *zucchini* blossom (*fiori di zucca*), orange flowers that can be fried in a thin coating of batter. Bigger *zucchini* can be stuffed (try spinach and ricotta).

Cucumber (*cetrioli*)

Most are short, fat and stubby with knobbly skins that need peeling and biggish seeds.

Fennel (*finocchio*)

Fennel grows in central regions, a member of the parsley family, a pale green tubular with a squat swollen root with stalks growing upwards and sprouting wispy green leaves. It peels like an onion, with a crisp texture like celery and a taste of aniseed. Cut up raw for salads, or braise. Used in fish dishes (lie whole fish on a bed of fennel and bake). The flat, elongated variety is stringier and not so good raw in salads. In Umbria they chop up the stalks and leaves and mix with garlic to make a stuffing for roast suckling pig. Wild fennel seeds (*cardoncelli*) are also used in cooking.

Fennel

French beans (*fagiolini verdi*)

These are lovely cold in summer salads, or served warm on

their own with a vinaigrette. Choose small young beans, bright green in colour and firm enough to snap in half. Top and tail and boil.

Garlic (*aglio*)

Italian cooking uses less garlic than French, except in dishes like the Genoese *pesto*. It is used more in the south than in the north. It is essential for fish soups or simply fried with olive oil as a sauce for spaghetti. You can buy garlic in bunches or plaits. Avoid dry and wrinkled looking cloves. Colour should be white, pink or mauve — not yellow.

Jerusalem artichokes (*topinambur*)

These hard knobbly roots grow in northern Italy in Piedmont and Friuli. The name comes from *girasole* sunflower. You buy them like potatoes, but look for smooth ones to make peeling easier. An autumn and winter vegetable, boil and purée for soups, or eat with butter — slightly sweet tasting.

Lamb's lettuce (*pasqualina, dolcetta*)

The leaves are tongue shaped, crispy green and used in salads. Limp leaves will perk up in a bowl of water.

Mushrooms (*funghi*)

You can hunt for the many varieties of wild mushrooms in late summer and early autumn, but you have to know what you're looking for. In the markets you'll find many different sorts: the fan-shaped *gallinacci*, large chunky *spugnole*, ridged *pineroli*, orange skinned *ovoli* (use raw in salads) and the expensive *porcini* (dark brown with large sticky heads). You can buy *porcini* dried (*secchi*) in little bags, their flavour intensifies as they cook. Soak them in warm water and then add to soups and sauces.

Onions (*cipolle*)

As you go further south, garlic gets substituted for onions in

Onions

recipes. Skins can be white, red or purple. Most are much sweeter than the onions we are used to and have a mild flavour. Some can be quite bitter like the *lampasciuni* from Apulia and the *cipuddazzi* from Calabria.

Peppers (*peperoni*)

Red, yellow or green, peppers add colour to any dish. Used extensively in the south where they are lightly fried with tomatoes (see p.149) into a *peperonata*, the large bell-shaped variety are often stuffed and then baked: *alla Napolitana* are with olives, capers and anchovies. *Peperonicino* (*rosso*) are hot red chillies.

Peppers

Radicchio

Radicchio is a root chicory with a slightly bitter taste that adds colour to salads. It is best in winter. Grown in the Veneto; the Treviso variety is red or white with elongated leaves, it is often served grilled with olive oil and salt and pepper. Also from Verona (shorter leaves and a round heart), and Castelfranco where the green leaves are speckled with red spots and streaks.

Radicchio

Radishes (*ravanelli*)

In the markets in winter and spring, the tiny ones are the sweetest. Wash the green leafy tops for salads.

Salsify (*sassefrica*)

First cultivated in the sixteenth century and used as a medicinal herb, salsify has long thin roots with white or black (*scorzonera*) skins, and is in the markets in autumn and winter. Peel or scrape and boil until tender. Remove woody centre in larger roots. Buy firm, not shrivelled or flabby.

Spinach (*spinaci*)

Young spinach leaves are delicious raw and shredded into salads. Much is grown in Florence, hence dishes *à la Fiorentina* (on a bed of spinach). Wash leaves well to remove mud. Use to stuff ravioli.

Tomatoes (*pomodori*)

Named by a sixteenth-century Sienese physician, *pomi d'oro* or golden apples on account of the first tomatoes that arrived from the Aztecs being yellow. The milder Italian sun brought out the pink in the pigment. For cooking the best are the San Marzano plum-shaped variety that ripen early. Ask for *pomodori da sugo* for sauces. Also in the south you'll see bunches of small cherry tomatoes (*sangiovannino*) hanging out to dry. When they're brought inside and hung up they last for a year. Round tomatoes are used for stuffing, soak them for half an hour in cold water, slice off the top and scoop out the pulp. Canned tomatoes are usually peeled (*pelati*) and used in sauces and soups, and you can buy tubes of tomato purée and jars of tomato sauces (with added ingredients).

Tomatoes

Truffles (*tartufi*)

This is not the chocolate but a very expensive delicacy, a bit like a mushroom. It is hunted out in oakwoods by special dogs (used to be pigs) from October to March. Truffles are grown in Tuscany, Emilia Romagna, Umbria and Piedmont. A whole truffle will grace the table of the most elegant dining rooms with a special truffle cutter for finely grating a sliver over the top of a cheese *fonduta* (Piedmont), or risotto, home-made *tagliolini*, eggs, salads, or chicken breasts. In Florence they are puréed into sandwiches in exclusive cafes; in Turin they grow to enormous proportions and in Piedmont they preserve them for two or three weeks in a jar of rice. The best ones are grey (*il grigio d'Alba*) or black (*il nero*), from Umbria. You may also find them in *salame*.

8

EXTRAS: STAPLES AND SUNDRIES HERBS, NUTS AND SPICES

STAPLES AND SUNDRIES

Anchovies (*alici, acciughe*)

Italians use a lot of anchovies in cooking: to top pizzas, in salads, stuffings and for a hot dip called *bagna cauda*, a speciality of the Piedmont. Salt-cured fillets are sold loose by weight in large drums. Choose from a newly opened drum if you can as the fillets at the top will be less salty than the ones at the bottom. Rinse under the tap, open the fillets and remove the bone then towel dry. Anchovies are also sold in tins and in tubes as a paste.

Beans (*fagioli*)

Most Italian beans came from Mexico and Central America in the sixteenth century. You can buy dried beans out of sacks in the markets and in summer you can buy them in their pods. Most dried beans will need soaking for twelve hours or so in warm water. Don't oversoak them as they will begin to ferment and sprout. After the soaking time is up, throw out any that are still floating, and throw away the water. Add fresh water and simmer gently until they are tender. Chickpeas (*ceci*) are used a great deal dried, particularly in south-

Chickpeas

ern Italy where they are a staple dish of Sicily. They are often puréed for soups, and although they need soaking you can buy them pre-soaked in grocers' shops. Seasoned with salt, pepper and soaked in olive oil they make a delicious salad. In Sardinia, Piedmont and Genoa, they make a thick pancake called *faina* or *farinata* made from the flour and cooked in oil in a wood oven. Slices are sold off barrows in winter and in special shops. Red or speckled *borlotti* beans, are used traditionally in the north and far south (for *minestrone*), while central Italy uses the small, white cannellini beans — delicious served warm soaked in olive oil, or in a thick *pasta e fagiole* soup.

Cannellini beans

Breadcrumbs (*Pangrattato*)

A lot of recipes call for breadcrumbs (for sprinkling over baked fish, for coating veal escalopes, etc.). Rather than make them yourself you can buy them in bags from local bakers.

Butter (*burro*)

Most butter sold in Italy is unsalted. Buy in supermarkets or in *alimentari*.

Cream (*panna, crema*)

You won't find many dishes that use cream, except in the north around Bologna. Whipped cream (*panna montata*) is used a lot in cakes, on top of ice-cream, *granita* and desserts. *Mascherpone* (*mascarpone*) is a cross between cream and cream cheese. It is sold thickly whipped and fresh and you can then sweeten it with sugar, brandy, or a liqueur. Try it on top of chestnut purée. Cream is sold in supermarkets and dairies (*latteria*), but you cannot get it delivered to your door!

Eggs (*uova*)

You can buy eggs in supermarkets or in shops that sell chickens and rabbits (*polleria* or *pollame*). Often they are smaller than the ones we get here and the yolks may be more orange. Free-range eggs are called *uova fresche* but the freshest are called *uova da bere*. Italian mamas whip them up for their sons with a drop of Marsala for breakfast — said to cure hangovers and the like. Look out for quails' eggs and pigeons' eggs in *salumeria* and supermarkets.

Flour (*farina*)

You won't be able to buy self-raising flour, Italians use baking powder for cakes. Soft plain flour (*grana tenera*) is used for cakes, *gnocchi* and bread. Harder flour (*farina tipo OO*) is used for pizzas and pasta if you can't get hold of *farina di semolo* (semolina flour) or *farina di grano duro* (durum wheat). You buy the raising agent separately. For bread or pizza buy sachets of *lievito per torte salate*, for sweet things like cakes, buy *lieveto per dolci*. *Fecola di patate* (potato flour) is also used for making cakes and biscuits. In Tuscany they use chestnut flour to bake their biscuits and cakes.

Milk (*latte*)

No morning deliveries I'm afraid. Buy it in *latteria* or supermarkets in plastic bottles and cartons. *Intero* is full cream, *pastorizzato* normal pasteurised, *parzialmente scremeto* is semi-skimmed and *scremeto* is skimmed.

Oil (*olio*)

Although olive oil (*olio d'oliva*) is used almost exclusively in cooking and salads particularly in the south, Tuscany, Liguria and Piedmont, it can be a bit rich to start with. Alternatives are peanut oil (*arachide*) or sunflower seed oil (*olio di sasso*). Both are also cheaper.

Quality is very important, but although Italy produces the best olive oil in the world that doesn't mean that every bottle you buy will be a good one. The light golden colour oils will be less strong than the heavy green variety which have a distinctive flavour.

The best olive oils come from Lucca in Tuscany, Liguria and from Sassari in Sardinia. Ligurian olive oil is generally whiter and lighter than oil from the small hand-picked olives of Tuscany. These produce a thick green oil that tastes a bit peppery. In the south the trees grow much bigger and the olives are usually allowed to drop to the ground. The oil is heavier, greasier and a golden colour.

The quality of the oil depends on: the crop of olives in any one year, the farm and the variety. Usually the smaller olives are used to make the oil, the bigger ones get eaten. The harvest begins around November and lasts for a good few months, involving whole villages in the daily picking and pressing. Everything, including the stones, goes into the oil. At the local *frantoio* on smaller farms in Tuscany the olives are ground into a paste between two stone wheels and then stacked on coconut fibre mats with spiked bases. A hydraulic press separates out the best oil and the rest goes to a factory for a hot water treatment and a second pressing.

For the best olive oil look for cold pressed extra virgin oil (*extra vergine*). Extra virgin means less than 1 per cent acidity. *Sopraffino*, fine virgin and virgin may have acidity up to 4 per cent. You're most likely to find the best oil in the place of production or by the roadside outside it. Once it leaves the farm it is rare to find 100 per cent pure virgin oil — even in the farm you may be fobbed off with last year's oil.

The second pressing, the one that goes to the commercial factory is blended with other, inferior oils, and ends up in supermarkets.

In Tuscany virtually every dish uses olive oil. To sample it at its best, buy a *filone* (a thick crusty farmer's loaf) sold at the local baker's shop to make a *fettaunta*. Cut it into thick slices, toast it on the stove or over a flame, take a clove of garlic and rub it on and then pour olive oil over it.

Keep your olive oil out of the sun and in a dark place. It doesn't keep terribly well. It isn't particularly cheap but the best is well worth taking home.

Olives (*olive*)

Olives in Italy aren't just saved for guests at a cocktail party but used in numerous dishes, particularly in the south. There are umpteen varieties, sizes and colours: yellow, black, green, purple among them. Of the green olives the small oval ones are considered the best. Black olives are used most in southern cooking. If you're using them in an *antipasto* choose

Olives

small ones as the larger ones can be saltier. The skins tend to be smooth before they're salted, and wrinkle and begin to yellow when they are left in brine. Size is no indication of quality. To store, put them in a jar with a little olive oil.

Rice (*riso*)

Rice was once a very valuable commodity and in the eighteenth century it was illegal to export even a grain. Italians still regard it very highly especially in the north where it is a staple food. One of the most famous dishes is *risotto alla Milanese* (rice cooked slowly in chicken stock and saffron, see p. 142). If you're buying rice to make risotto you will need the round grain variety called Arborio.

Semolina (*semolino*)

Used for the baby and to make *gnocchi*, semolina is coarse-grained particles of durum wheat — in fact what shop-bought pasta should be made of.

Tunny Fish in Oil (*tonno in scatola*)

It is always useful to have some tuna in your larder. In Italy you can buy it out of barrels like anchovies, by the kilo. Make sure if you are using it for a salad or with say, pimentoes, boiled potatoes, or french beans that you buy the best quality. Ask for *ventresca*, which is the tender stomach, rather than the cheaper variety which is fine for sauces or stuffings.

Vinegar (*aceto*)

Wine vinegar, either red or white, is used most in vinaigrettes, and for cooking. Italians also use a strong *balsamico* vinegar, an infusion of herbs and the 'musts' of grapes. They often put a few drops on meat before grilling it to bring out the flavour.

HERBS, NUTS AND SPICES

It was Marco Polo who was responsible for introducing spices to Italy by opening up a direct trading route to the Far East. Venetian merchants quickly cornered the market, buying spices cheaply and selling them at exorbitant prices, building their palaces with the profits. The fall of Constantinople in 1453 closed the route to the Far East, but the Venetians continued trading with Moslems in the Near East until Portugal discovered the Spice Islands and Lisbon became the centre of the spice trade. Italians have never lost their interest in spices and many are used in cooking.

Almonds

Almonds (*mandorle*)

Almonds are used extensively to make cakes, sweets and biscuits. Marzipan-shaped fruit is often sold in *pasticceria*.

Bay Leaves (*foglie d'alloro*)

You can help yourself virtually all year round to the stiff green leaves from this evergreen tree or bush. Soak them (one or two are usually enough to flavour soups, stews or sauces) for five minutes before using. To get a stronger flavour, mince up fresh leaves. Italians also use bay leaves boiled in a little milk for a sweet cream or a white sauce.

Basil (*basilico*)

One of the most important herbs in Italian cooking and essential with tomatoes, basil grows in great abandon along the Ligurian coast where it is used in *pesto Genoese* (see p. 151). Look out for the giant variety, *basilico a foglie di lattughe*, with leaves as big as lettuce. You might like to buy yourself a little pot and pick off leaves as you need them. Use fresh leaves, shredded as chopped spoils the flavour, in sauces, salads and soups. Sprinkle it over red mullet; blend it

Basil

with butter for steaks; or add to sweet peppers or aubergines/
eggplant.

Borage (*boraggine*)

Grows wild, especially in Liguria, the leaves are covered in
coarse hairs and the plant has sky blue flowers. Borage is one
of the herbs used in Pimms. In Italy they add it to wine cups,
use the leaves to stuff ravioli, boil them like spinach and even
fry them in batter.

Capers (*capperi*)

Capers grow in dry volcanic soil (Lipari, Apulia or in Sicily).
You can see the plants with their pink and white flowers
poking out of crevices in the rocks. The caper is the
unopened bud of the flower and it is preserved in vinegar. It
is used extensively on pizzas and in sauces. If they are too
strong or salty, rinse them before using.

Chestnuts (*marrone, castagne*)

Italian chestnuts are very versatile. They are puréed in soups,
served boiled with wild boar, pounded in stuffings and made
into delicious cakes and sweets. In former times the flour was
used to make bread. In winter you'll see them being roasted
over braziers in Rome and Florence, in summer they flavour
ice-cream. (See p.168 for a quick and easy chestnut and
chocolate cake.) If you can't be bothered to boil and peel
chestnuts yourself the puréed brands sold in jars are much
cheaper than any we can get at home — well worth bringing
back with you if you like them. Spoon out a few portions and
top with *mascarpone* cream as a delicious and simple
dessert. Also try marron glacé, sold loose in *pasticceria* —
very different from the often dried up fruits you find ready
boxed here.

Chestnuts

Cinnamon (*cannella*)

You can buy cinnamon powdered or in sticks. Use it to flavour cakes and puddings, meat and game dishes and *ricotta* cheese.

Cloves (*chiodi di garofano*)

Used in *panforte di Siena*, a spiced cake, and in some meat and game dishes.

Coriander Seeds (*coriandolo*)

These are used for flavouring roast lamb or pork.

Fennel Seeds (*semi di finocchio*)

Fennel seeds have an aniseed flavour and are the ingredient used to spice *finocchiona* — the Florentine *salame*, and dried figs fromn Bari. Try sprinkling them into fish or chicken dishes.

Juniper (*ginepro*)

The berries have a bitter and aromatic taste. Juniper grows wild in mountain and inland areas and is used to marinate wild boar, pork and venison and for stuffings for pork, mutton and game.

Marjoram (wild) (*origano*)

Oregano and wild marjoram are closely related; marjoram being slightly milder. The Italians call it all *origano* and use it a lot on pizza, and in tomato sauces. You can buy it in bundles in the markets or help yourself from the hillsides and hang it out in your kitchen to dry. Sweet marjoram (*massiorana*) is used in soups, stews and fish dishes.

Mint (*menta*)

Mint grows wild and looks rather like basil. Use it to freshen your drinks and in soups (see p.130). *Mentuccia* or *menta Romana* is peppermint. The flavour is aromatic rather than minty and you can scatter fresh leaves into vegetable or fish dishes, into salads or soups. It is also good with fresh *porcini* mushrooms.

Myrtle (*mirto*)

Myrtle grows wild. In Sardinia you'll even see it on the beach. It is an evergreen with straight twigs, stiff leaves and purple black berries in summer. The flowers are white. It belongs to the heather family and its perfume in the early evening fills the air. Sprigs are wrapped around baby pig (*porceddu*) and small birds, roast thrush or blackbird (*taccula*) are often put in little bags of myrtle leaves to absorb the flavour.

Nutmeg (*noce moscata*)

Use a pinch in stews, soups and white sauces. In Italy you can buy it as a whole 'nut', and use a special grater. If you haven't got one, just chip a bit off with a knife.

Oregano (*origano*)

See Marjoram.

Parsley (*prezzemolo*)

Said to have originated in Sardinia, the Italian variety has feathery flat leaves rather than the tight curls we're familiar with. The stem is milder than the leaf. Italians chop it up with garlic for sauces, use it in soups, stews and stuffings.

Pine Nuts (*pinoli*)

These are the pellets inside pine cones. The cones are gathered in November and stored until the summer sun comes out when they are put out to dry. The seeds can then be shaken out and cracked. Inside the black pellet is a creamy white kernel which is delicious raw or chopped up in stuffings and sauces. They are used in the Genoese *pesto* in meat, fish and game dishes, in stuffings for pasta and in sweets. You can buy them in little packets and they are much cheaper in Italy than here.

Rocket (*rucola, ruchetta, rughetta*)

Rocket is a dandelion-shaped leaf with a nutty, slightly bitter flavour, used in green salads. It has a yellowish edible flower and the leaves smell when bruised.

Rosemary (*rosmarino*)

This herb grows wild in bushes by the roadside and in the hills. It can grow up to six feet high and is one of the most common aromatic plants in the Mediterranean with pale blue flowers. You can smell it in the early evening and as it roasts in the midday sun. Help yourself and sprinkle it on roast lamb and roast suckling pig, on chicken, baked or grilled fish, potatoes (see p.149), or, like the Italians, on roast beef. In markets or in butchers' shops you may see meat already wrapped in the spiky stems, ready for roasting.

Saffron (*zafferano*)

Saffron is very expensive. The saffron crocus grows in the Abruzzi and in Sardinia and comes from the pistils in the autumn flowers. There are only three to each flower which accounts for the high cost — and forgeries. If you can, buy the actual pistils rather than the powder and soak in a little water. One of the principal dishes saffron is used in is *risotto alla Milanese*, and it's also delicious in fish soup.

Sage (*salvia*)

Buy it fresh. The leaves are slightly furry and a grey green colour. Keep them airtight and use in roasts and with veal and liver.

Salt (*sale*)

Italy's salt comes from salt lagoons on the Aeolian Islands (Salina) and from Cagliari on Sardinia. It is sold in delicatessens and tobacconists' shops as it is a state monopoly. *Sale grosso* are flakes, and *sale fine da tavola* is table salt.

Thyme (*timo*)

Buy it fresh in sprigs; the tiny leaves are used to flavour grilled fish, tomato sauces and meats.

9
LOCAL CHEESES

CHEESE (*FORMAGGIO*)

Italians love cheese and claim even more varieties than France! Cheese is used a great deal in cooking from the gooey *mozzarella* that tops the southern pizzas to the hard, granular Parmesan from Emilia Romagna in the north, that's grated over pasta.

Other cheeses most used in recipes are *pecorino* which is a hard cheese made from sheep's milk, with a sharper flavour than Parmesan; the soft and almost tasteless *ricotta* which is often used in sweets, particularly cheesecake which the Romans claim to have invented and *fontina*, which is melted to make the *fonduta* of the Piedmont, a fondue served with sliced truffles on the top.

Each region makes its own cheeses, much is made on a small scale by individual farmers who produce cheeses of very high quality. The *casaro* is a true artisan and his cheeses are usually made by the whole family, with the skill passed down from father to son. Move outside the region and you probably won't find the same cheese anywhere else in the world.

About a third of the entire milk output of cows, sheep, goats and buffalo (where the best *mozzarella* comes from) goes into cheese production. The greatest amount of cheese is made in Lombardy, followed by Emilia Romagna, the Veneto and Piedmont. Top of the sales are the hard *grana* cheeses, like *parmigiano-reggiano*, and *provolone*, made by co-operatives. Factory-made cheeses like Bel Paese, find their way onto supermarket shelves here.

It is best to keep the soft creamy cheeses in the fridge if it is hot (in high summer you may not find some cheeses, like *mascarpone* in the shops) and the hard granular cheeses too. Wrap them tightly in silver foil.

A few words which get attached to named cheeses are:

Affumicato	Smoked
Caprino	Made from goat's milk
Dolce	Sweet
Maggengo	A milano or *grana* cheese made from April to September
Mezzanello	A young cheese
Nostrano	Local
Pecorino	Made from sheep's milk
Piccante	Sharp
Quartirolo	The same cheese as *maggengo*. Made from September to November
Stravecchio	A very old and strong cheese
Terzolo and *Invernengo*	The same cheese as *maggengo* made in winter from different pastures
Vacchino	Made from cow's milk
Vecchio	An older cheese with a stronger flavour

The following are just some of the cheeses you might come across:

Asiago (Veneto) One of the region's most famous cheeses from Asiago at the foot of the Dolomites and elsewhere. This straw coloured cheese with holes has a mild flavour and a smooth rind. *Asiago Pressato* is similar. The older cheese is used for grating and has a strong smell.

Asin (north) A white curd cheese, made on farms in the mountains, eaten as a dessert with fruit or honey.

Bel Paese A trade name meaning 'beautiful country'. A creamy, mild soft cheese that comes in round individual portions wrapped in foil, children love it on rolls. In cooking it is used as a substitute for *mozzarella*.

Bitto (north) Firm cheese, similar to *Fontina*.

Bra (Piedmont) Hard cheese that's been around for centuries, nearly white, sharp and salty.

Caciocavalla A firm cheese used for cooking that takes its name from its shape. The curd is formed into large oval shapes that are tied together in pairs and hung over a piece of wood. Similar to *provolone*.

Caciota Lots of different types, most are mild and soft with a few holes.

Castelmagno Similar to *Gorgonzola* with a blue mould.

Crescenza Like *Bel Paese*, soft and slightly creamy, rectangular-shaped, white and rindless.

Dolcelatte You probably won't find it in Italy as it is made for the export market. Blander and milder than *Gorgonzola* but looks similar, greeny blue veins, should be slightly runny when ripe.

Fiore Sarde (Sardinia) A hard mild cheese made from sheep's milk with a dark yellow rind. Used for grating.

Fontina A mountain cheese from the Aosta Valley in the Piedmont, a creamy, pale cheese with a reddish brown crust. Used a lot in cooking, grated onto soups, and *polenta*, also melted to make the Piedmont dish called *fonduta* served with white truffles.

Formaggi di Pasta Filata This is a generic name for a group of cheeses made by curdling milk with rennet, fermenting it and then shaping it so that it's free of holes. It keeps well even in warm climates. Cheeses include: *provolone, caciocavallo, mozzarella, provatura* and *scamorze.*

Gorgonzola Famous blue veined cheese from north-east of Milan said to have been made in the Po Valley since AD 879. Cured in caves in the Alps. Keep covered as it loses its flavour in the air. *Torte di mascarpone* is a heavy rich cheese: It consists of layers of *mascarpone* and *Gorgonzola*.

Grana Generic name for cheeses with a granular texture, developed by the Etruscans, 2500 years ago. Used for grating over pasta. Do not slice but break off bits. Keeps airtight in a cool place. The best of the *grana* cheeses is *grana pedano* which will be written in red ink horizontally over the rind.

Mascarpone (mascherpone) Thick fresh cream cheese sold in white muslin parcels and used in desserts in place of whipped cream. A bit like *ricotta* but creamier and much richer. Bland, so add sugar, cinnamon, liqueur or fruit. Italian children eat it for tea with an egg yolk and sugar beaten into it. Delicious over chestnut purée or melted as a sauce for *ravioli* with walnuts.

Milano Soft cheese from Lombardy like *Bel Paese*, may be wrapped in muslin.

Montasio Like *fontina* from Friuli and the Veneto, sometimes the rind is blackened with soot. Strongish flavour, soft with a few holes.

Mozzarella The best *mozzarella* is still made from water buffalo's milk (*bufalina*). It is whiter than the cow's milk variety and tastes chewier. It is almost sacrilege to cook with it: slice it on a plate with tomatoes onto which you've sprinkled some good olive oil and fresh basil. Cow's milk *mozzarella* is available everywhere and usually called *fior di latte*. It is used a lot in cooking: for topping pizzas; for melting on top of veal escalopes fried in egg and breadcrumbs (*Milanese*); for vegetables dishes like *melanzane alla parmigiana* (see p.147) and for frying with bread (*in carrozza* — see p.136).

All *mozzarella* is porcelain white in colour, very smooth and comes in small rounds swimming in their own whey in which it should be kept. It should be eaten as fresh as possible. You can also buy it smoked (*affumicato*) with a golden skin, egg shaped (*uova di bufalo*) and plaited (*treccia*).

The best comes from Naples where the water buffaloes graze on the flat marshy plains around the River Sele. South of Naples you can visit dairies where it is made. One, called the Caseificio Valtusciano, is at Battipaglia on the road from Salerno to Paestum.

Parmigiano-Reggiano (Parmesan) The best of the grating cheeses, known outside Italy as Parmesan and inside Italy as *grana*. To the Italians it is as valuable as gold dust and in times of inflation they have been known to store great drums of it in the bank! It is expensive but a little goes a long way. You buy it in a wedge and grate it yourself over pasta, and soups. It is also delicious on its own to nibble, with a glass of good red wine.

It should be pale yellow, not grey, and there is no substitute for the real thing which has its name stamped in vertical lines all over the gold or dark coloured rind.

Real *parmigiano* bears no resemblance whatsoever to the white manufactured powder you get already grated in supermarkets here. To stop it oxidising chalk is added. The taste is literally the difference between chalk and cheese.

To keep chunks of *parmigiano* fresh, wrap it in silver paper and store in the bottom of the fridge. The colour should stay pale yellow. If it lightens wrap it in a damp cloth (muslin is best) and then the foil and leave it overnight in the

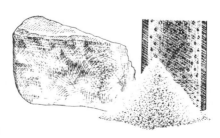

Parmesan

fridge. In the morning take off the cloth. If you have grated some and there is any left over leave it on an open saucer, but it will only last three or four days.

Pecorino Generic name for sheep's milk cheese, most of it still made by hand on small farms (*pecora* is Italian for sheep). A strong, salty cheese with a white rind. Eat it with fruit or in a salad as an *antipasto*. Also used for grating. Usually worth trying wherever you are.

Provatura Soft cheese from southern Italy, looks like a *caciocavallo*.

Provolone Plastic curd cheese like *caciocavallo*, made like *mozzarella* except that the curds ferment for longer and the cheese ends up much bigger: a *provolone giganti* can be as big as 200 lbs. It comes in all sorts of other shapes and sizes too. Used in cooking and loved by children in sandwiches and snacks.

Ragusano (Sicily) Used for grating, the grooved surface is made by the string it is hung on to ripen.

Ricotta A byproduct of cheese made from the whey. The genuine cheese is made from sheep's milk. A mild, totally bland cheese that doesn't keep well. In southern Italy they add salt and drain it, forming it into a solid cheese a bit like the Greek *feta*. Usually eaten with something else, like fruit, or cooked (try it with spinach as a sauce for pasta), or in a cheesecake. Children usually like it.

Robbiola A soft, rich cheese like *crescenza*, made in the Alps, circular and flat.

Romano Popular, hard, grating cheese originally from Latium, now made in southern Italy and Sardinia.

Sardo Like *romano*, hard cheese used for grating.

Scarmorze Small, soft, mild cheese (*pasta filata*), originally made from buffalo's milk. A bit salty, Italians eat it toasted on bread or fried with an egg. Also smoked. Shaped like *caciocavallo*, larger ones come in nets.

Stracchino Generic name for several, rindless, soft cheeses (*crescenza* is one of the best). Produced by cows who leave the mountains in September and October to winter in the valleys of Lombardy. The 'tired' (*stracco*) cows produce good cheeses, *Gorgonzola* is one of them.

Taleggio (Lombardy) Soft cheese like *stracchino* with a thin pink mouldy rind, brick shaped and slightly aromatic.

Toma (Piedmont) A variety of different cheeses, smooth, slightly holey, firm and yellow in colour, the best are from the high mountains.

10
PASTA, PIZZA AND BREAD

PASTA

*When Yankee Doodle came to town riding on a pony,
he stuck a feather in his cap and called it macaroni.*

Spaghetti, lasagne, tagliatelle, agnellotti, capellini ... pasta is
the general name for all sorts of shapes and sizes of Italy's
national dish. It's been around for centuries and probably
originated in the Middle East when caravan drivers who
crossed the desert carrying spices decided they needed something that would keep a bit longer than bread to take with
them on their long journeys. They concocted a paste with
water, dried it out and then cut it into strips, bringing it back
to life by cooking it in water.

The Arabs were one of the first settlers in Sicily and soon
their *trii* (the Arab word for string) caught on on the mainland. Marco Polo changed the name to *lasagne*, then, for a
while it was called *maccheroni*, followed by *fidelini* — a word
with Spanish origins (they still call it *fideos* in Spain).

For about three centuries from 1500 to 1800 it was
known as *vermicelli* or 'little worms' then it was back to
maccheroni again, a word which, to the rest of the world
became synonymous with Italy. One way of, discreetly, telling
your friends you'd been to Italy was to serve *maccheroni* at
your dinner table. In the eighteenth century, 'Macaroni'
became a nickname for an Englishman who, back from his
travels to Italy sported not only a few Italian habits and affect-
ations but also an elaborate wig 'he stuck a feather in his cap
and called it macaroni!' The 'he' was an English dandy who
from then on became known as a Macaroni. Not that he
seemed to mind particularly. Macaronis founded their own

exclusive club, and presumably wore their feathers in their hats to visit it!

There are all sorts of stories about how various other types of pasta got their names. *Ravioli* originated in Liguria and its name comes from the Genoese *robiole* meaning 'things of no importance' — leftovers that were stuffed into envelopes of pasta for sailors to take out to sea with them.

The Neapolitans were responsible for mating *maccheroni* with the tiny, cherry-sized tomato which was brought from Mexico and Peru in the sixteenth century, and in the nineteenth century visitors from abroad and even other regions were so impressed with the pasta dishes they ate that they took some home with them as a souvenir.

As the popularity of pasta grew so did new shapes, and they are still being invented.

A couple of years ago Giorgetto Giugiaro, an industrial designer more at home designing aerodynamics for cars than inventing types of pasta, was commissioned to design a new shape for spaghetti! After months at the drawing board he came up with what looked a bit like a wave. He called it *marille* (after *mare*, the sea). It is now selling well, possibly because a plateful of *marille* only contains half the calories of a plate of spaghetti.

Pasta is most certainly fattening, but that doesn't seem to stop Italians enjoying it.

More pasta is eaten in the south of Italy than in central or northern parts. In the south they eat a lot more of the tubular, factory-made pasta, while in the north and centre they often prefer to make their own. There's absolutely nothing wrong with buying ready-made pasta, Italians do it, so there's no reason why you shouldn't, especially if you don't fancy spending hours rolling out dough.

There's such a lot you can do with pasta that doesn't involve hours in the kitchen. In the poorer regions they eat spaghetti with olive oil and garlic, you can serve it with a little *ricotta* cheese, broccoli or spinach; with flaked tuna; small zucchini/courgettes which have been fried in a little olive oil; or with clams in a tomato sauce — virtually anything goes. Ideally different shapes of pasta go with different sauces. In general Italians eat long pasta with tomato, fish, cream and heavy sauces like *pesto*. The short, hollow variety like *macaroni* or *fusilli* usually have heavier, meaty sauces or plain tomato, butter and grated Parmesan.

Stuffed pastas (*ravioli* etc.) which you can buy ready made, don't really need a sauce. All you have to do is boil them for a minute or two and serve with a blob of butter and freshly grated Parmesan cheese. Sauces in jars and bottles are usually good in Italy, especially if you stick to a well-known brand like Barilla, or Buitoni. You can make yourself a real *pesto*, or spend time cleaning out *vongole* (clams) or you can buy a tin. Sitting out in the sunshine, only you will probably know the difference!

Buying Pasta

Factory-made, dried pasta (*pasta compra*) is available in all supermarkets and grocers' shops. There will be hundreds of different shapes and sizes to choose from. Look for the words *semola di grano duro* (durum semolina or wheat) on the packet and you'll be buying the best quality. Buy pasta that is yellow, rather than grey. The green variety will be flavoured with spinach, the red with tomato. Pasta made in Naples is supposed to be better than pasta produced in other parts of Italy, on account of the superiority of the water!

Home-made pasta can be bought in bigger towns and villages. It is, of course, more expensive. You may be able to get it in the bread shop (*panettiere* or *fornaio*) or in special *pasta fresca* shops or *rosticceria*. Sheets of pasta are in great demand in Emilia Romagna, for example, where they special-ise in dishes like *lasagne*, while in Rome you can buy *fettu-cine* — even the restaurants buy it freshly made from the shop around the corner. Pasta is also sold flavoured with basil or chocolate. There is no great kudos to be gained by making your own.

Pasta — *fusilli, ravioli, pappardelle* and *marille*

To keep fresh pasta either cover it with a damp cloth or allow it to dry out on a dish, uncovered, in a cool place. It will keep for about a month. Once it has dried it will take longer to cook and can be stored in a jar. Keep stuffed *ravioli* in the fridge.

Cooking Pasta

Factory-made pasta takes a lot longer to cook than home-made pasta, but not necessarily as long as it says on the packet. It is easy to turn pasta into a soggy mess. The secret of making pasta lies in the timing and the water.

Allow 3 ounces (90g) of pasta per person as a first course, 4 ounces (120g) as a main course.

Factory-made pasta will swell up more than home-made pasta. Both will need 4 litres (7 pints) of water to every 1lb (500g).

Bring the water to the boil and add a heaped tablespoon (optional) of salt to every pound. Add all the pasta at once, try not to snap long spaghetti, it will bend as it hits the water. Stir with a wooden spoon to stop it sticking. Cover the pan until the water comes to the boil again and then take the lid off and cook gently.

Factory-made pasta, depending on the thickness and shape, may need as long as fifteen minutes. Allow for the fact that it will continue to cook when you're draining it. Keep watching and lift out a little on a fork to taste. It is ready when you can bite into it without snapping it, although Italians like their pasta *al dente* with a bite and we're used to eating it softer. Drain quickly in a colander or sieve, shaking the excess water out. Try not to lift too many strands in the air as it will get cold. Add butter before the sauce and serve straight away.

Should you have any left over there are several Italian pasta salads which make use of it cold.

Cooking home-made pasta involves the same process only it takes less time. Fresh, flat pasta takes only seconds, long *tagliatelle* minutes. You might as well get everybody sitting down as soon as you put it into the water.

Pasta Glossary

Agnolotti	Largish, crescent-shaped envelopes stuffed with meat
Aglio e olio	Oil and garlic
Agnolini	Small ravioli
Al dente	The way Italians like their pasta, firm with a bite
Amatriciana	Sauce of tomatoes, hot pepper and salted pork, from Piedmont
Anellini	Tiny pasta rings for soup
Cannelloni	Tubes of pasta, stuffed with meat and a bechamel sauce
Capellini	Very thin spaghetti

Cappelletti	Hat shaped, stuffed with meat and cheese, from Emilia Romagna
Carbonara	Sauce of eggs, bacon and pepper
Conchiglie	Shells
Fettuccine	Roman version of tagliatelle
Fusilli	Twisted spirals
Gnocchi	Open shell shapes
Lumachelle	Like land snails
Maccheroni	Small tubes and once common name for all pasta
Maltagliati	Badly cut, used for soups
Marille	New, wave-shaped spaghetti
Orecchiette	Ear shaped
Pappardelle	Broad egg noodles
Pastina	Little pasta for broth
Penne	Elongated quills
Pesto	Strong sauce from Liguria made from basil, garlic and pine nuts
Quadrucci	Little squares used in broth
Ragu	Meat sauce with vegetables
Ravioli	Envelopes stuffed with meat, fish or cheese
Rigatoni	Short ridged, cylindrical, chewy pipes
Spaghetti	Long strands of pasta
Tagliatelle	Long, thin, flat noodles made with eggs
Tagliolini	Thin noodles for soups
Tortellini	Tiny belly button shapes stuffed, used in soups
Tortelloni	Large squares, stuffed
Zite	Cone shapes

PIZZA

Pizza was a staple ancient Roman breakfast. Italians don't often cook it at home, probably because it is so much better in pizzerias.

You can buy pizzas cut up into squares from *fornaio* or *rosticceria*, *calzone* are folded over with the filling in the middle, or take away or eat your pizza in restaurants up and down the country.

You'll find the most toppings in southern Italy, anything and everything eventually finds its way onto a pizza. In Naples the best is the simplest: topped with fresh tomatoes, *mozzarella* cheese and some good olive oil.

It is unlikely that you will want to bake your own on holiday — there's no better or cheaper meal than to go to the nearest pizzeria, order a bottle of wine and wait for your pizza (the big ones are enormous) to emerge from a brick oven. You can usually watch the dough being stretched and the toppings go on — quite an interesting experience for children.

BREAD

Italians love bread and there are thousands of different types of loaves, sometimes sweet, sometimes savoury — each region has its own. Almost every village has a *panettiere, panificio* or *fornaio* — where bread is baked fresh, usually twice a day, and you can buy it still warm from the oven.

Italians take their bread more seriously than we do, and eat a lot of it, on its own, in soups, toasted and in salads. It would be impossible to describe all the different breads. Here are a few of the more interesting ones:

Focaccia is a thin crusty bread that makes a good snack; Italian children take it to school. You can buy squares of it, warm, from the local baker. While it is most commonly flavoured with salt, you can get *focaccia* made with anything — bacon, onions, sage, herbs, olives.

In Tuscany the bread is almost salt-free, a reminder of the time when the Pope put a levy on salt and the people decided to eat their bread without it rather than give him the money.

In Sicily they eat a *pagnotta 'mmiscata*, kneaded with pork fat, and spiked with pitted black olives and fresh *pecorino* cheese. The *'mpignulata* is made with a piquant sausage and oregano.

In Emilia Romagna the unleavened *piada* is a bit like a Mexican tortilla. Sardinia has a similar bread called *carta da musica* (see p. 137).

Several regions make *bruschetta*. Ask for a *pane casareccio*, a round white loaf (any white bread will do). Slice it and toast it and then rub it with garlic and olive oil and pop it in the oven. Bread is fried to make the tiny *crostini*, used in soups as croutons or spread with cheese, anchovies or liver. Crusts aren't wasted either. In the Piedmont they use them to mop up the splendid *fonduta* (cheese dip).

For breakfast, most bars sell warm *brioche* or *cornetti*, and *croissant*, filled with jam, a custardy cream or chocolate. Supermarkets sell sliced bread (*pan carre*) for toast. *Alimentari* sell filled rolls. You can also buy wholemeal bread (*pane integrale*) from most bakers and thin *grissini*, breadsticks, which children like.

11

CAKES, BISCUITS, ICES &SWEETS

CAKES, BISCUITS AND SWEETS

Italians don't go in for puddings very much but they do like cakes, sweets and chocolates, and biscuits which they dip into their sweet dessert wines.

Nuts play an important part in cakes and confectionery and Piedmont is the main supplier with its high quality chestnuts, and hazelnuts. Fruit, usually crystallised, and honey are the other essential ingredients.

The art of crystallising fruit goes back, like most Italian cooking, to ancient Rome, when fruit was encrusted with honey in the absence of sugar. Crystallised fruit and flowers from Genoa and Naples were on the banquet table of Henry IV when he married Maria di Medici in 1600. But it was Sicily's Arab rulers who were responsible for using candied fruit to its best effect, producing *cassata* and *cannoli* which are still popular today.

Marzipan made its debut in the fourteenth-century in a convent in Palermo, where the nuns modelled fruit out of almond paste. Much of Italy today prides itself on its marzipan products.

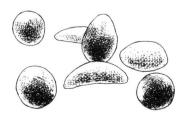

Marzipan shapes

93

Biscuits were known by the Romans as *panis nauticus* or shipbread, because they could be taken on board ships in large quantities and would remain fresh for a long time. These days the Veneto probably produces the best biscuits (see p. 166 for recipe for *Le bisse*).

There are hundreds of different cakes, sweets and biscuits. Each region has its own specialities. Here are a few worth looking out for.

Amaretti A macaroon wrapped in a thin twist of paper (light the paper with a match and watch it float up magically into the air). Made of bitter almonds and apricot seeds, it dates back to the 1700s. The most famous come in a red square tin from Saronno in Liguria.

Cannoli Sicily's famous cylindrical pastry rolls filled like a cassata and flavoured with vanilla or cream cheese, candied fruit and chocolate.

Cassata From Sicily, a sponge cake filled with sugar, candied fruit and covered with marzipan or chocolate icing.

Cassata

Cioccolate Chocolate is world famous from Turin. Look for: gold wrapped oblong-shaped Gianduia chocolates; *baci* (kisses) individually wrapped in silver foil, milk chocolates with chopped hazelnuts, each with an individual message under the wrapping; and pralines from Bologna.

Colomba Eaten at Easter, a dove-shaped yeast cake made with toasted chestnuts, rather like *Panettone*.

Confetti Sugared almonds encased in honey and flour originally from the Abruzzi. They are handed out at weddings like confetti. In former times in Rome the bridegroom would walk the streets the night before the wedding and shower the children with handfuls of walnuts (later became almonds) which they used for playing marbles!

Marrons Glacés Crystallised chestnuts, from Piedmont and Veneto, reputedly invented by Catherine de Medici. Sold loose or in boxes.

Mostarda Candied fruits (even eel!) in a mustard syrup, like chutney, and eaten with cold meat. Best from Cremona (where the great Stradivarius violins are made).

Panettone Possibly Italy's (Milan's) most familiar looking cake. Eaten at Christmas, a light yellow cake made with sultanas and candied peel with a domed shaped top, packed in large boxes that fill shop windows up and down the country. Motta and Alemagna are the biggest brands.

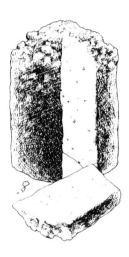

Panettone

Panforte Siena's answer to *Panettone*, a hard, flat cake originally made by monks in the Middle Ages. The classic cake was black and sweet, made with grapes or figs and honey then spices, cloves, cinnamon and pepper were added. These days it's white and made with a sweet dough flavoured with vanilla and candied fruits, covered with almond paste and coated with peel and roasted almonds. The best is freshly made by bakers and it should be soft and chewy.

Pandoro Verona's Christmas cake dates back to the Renaissance, a light, star-shaped sponge with a sprinkling of icing.

Parrozzo The Abruzzo peasant's rough bread, a chocolate covered bun. It originated in Pescara and is sold in a huge hexagonal box.

Torrone A gooey white bar of nougat with pieces of roasted almonds, walnuts or hazelnuts wedged into it, sometimes with dried figs and honey too. Called after the thirteenth-century *campanile* of Cremona, the Torrazzo — or if you prefer from the Latin *torrere* to roast. Eaten traditionally on Christmas Eve. Don't miss it. The best and freshest are sold in *pastic-*

ceria, rather than the commercially produced bars sold in supermarkets.

Zabaglione A frothy yellow pudding served warm in a glass, made with egg yolks, sugar and Marsala. Also served cold on cakes and in ice-cream.

Zuppa Inglese An English style trifle. Also a flavour of ice-cream.

ICE-CREAM

Italians claim to make the best ice-cream in the world. Even if it isn't there are certainly more varieties and flavours than you can possibly imagine.

Even the Romans ate it, in the form of snow carried down from the mountains and flavoured with the juice from fresh fruits. But it wasn't until the nineteenth century that ice-cream became an Italian obsession, enjoyed by a privileged few. In former times ice-cream was sold from three-wheeled carts, the ices kept out of the sunlight by a large umbrella. The vendor pedalled through the streets and into the parks where children screamed with delight as soon as they saw him. You can still see them in some parts of southern Italy although many now sell factory-made ice-cream.

Bars and *gelateria* sell home-made ice-cream. Look for signs that say *produzione propria*. As for flavours, in the summer months anything and everything flavours ice-cream: basil, coconut, *baci* chocolates, watermelon, peaches, pears, jasmine, liqueurs, chestnuts — over 20 per cent of Italy's entire fruit production goes into ice-cream.

Real Italian ice-cream is strictly controlled by law; even individuals who make it to sell on a small scale have to adhere to it. Which means that *gelato all'Italiana* not only tastes nice but has nutritious ingredients. Only buy ice-cream from a shop that looks as if it sells a lot of it — in the heat ices are a breeding ground for bacteria. If you are in doubt buy the packet variety. There are plenty of shapes that children won't know already.

In summer you can sit outside a bar for breakfast and have a *granita* (glass of crushed ice, flavoured with coffee or strawberries) *con panna*, with a blob of whipped cream on top. Or after dinner try a *cassata* (made with sweetened *ricotta* in Sicily). In the south children even eat ice-cream buns *brioche con gelato*. The glossary below might help you identify some of the main types:

Agrumi gelati Citrus fruit with the middle taken out and replaced with ice-cream flavoured with the juice and peel.

Bombe Spherical 'bombs' with layers of hard ice-cream and softer ice-cream in the centre, sometimes covered in pastry.

Caldo-freddo Vanilla ice-cream with hot chocolate or hot coffee.

Cassata Frozen version of a Sicilian dessert. Two or three layers of ice-cream, with a middle of *semi-freddo*, made with meringue, whipped cream and candied fruits cut into small strips.

Gelati General name for all ice-cream.

Gelato affogato Ice-cream 'drowned' in spirits: cognac, vodka or whisky.

Granita A crushed ice sorbet, a bit like a slushpuppy, flavoured with coffee, lemon, strawberries.

Semi-freddo Ice-cream made with eggs, meringue and whipped cream.

Sorbetto Sorbet made with syrup and fresh fruit juice or pulp. May be flavoured with liqueur or wine.

Spumone Light ice-cream sometimes made with whipped egg whites or fruit. Sometimes a mousse.

Tartufi Chocolate or zabaglione ice-cream wrapped in chocolate or chunks of almonds.

Torte gelato Ice-cream cake often soaked in liqueur, cut into layers and decorated with whipped cream and candied fruit.

12

WINES, SPIRITS AND OTHER DRINKS

Italy is the largest wine producer in the world, yet only about 15 years ago Chianti was the only Italian wine most of us had ever heard of.

The vine has been cultivated in Italy for some two and a half thousand years and wine flowed freely at the tables of the Greeks and Romans and down the throats of the world's greatest painters and poets.

The ancient Cretans called Italy Oenotria — the land of wine, probably because the Italian vine grows uncontrollably over Italy's hillsides. It is a peasant crop involving whole families and villages in its production, but it took the Italians a long time to export wine in any great quantity. There were quite a few setbacks in the early days; wars in which invading soldiers trampled the vines underfoot, and then a disease that attacked the roots and inhibited growth. And then when everything seemed to be going well and vast quantities of wine started to be produced, the Italians discovered that some of it wasn't viewed too highly by the rest of the world and much of it landed smack in the middle of the European wine lake.

Admittedly some Italian wine does have a reputation for being 'plonk'. As in France, a lot of areas merely produce a cheap drink for the locals, with no pretensions at all. Occasionally these rustic blends find their way abroad. Even the known names are not always as good as they ought to be. The Italians were a bit too enthusiastic about overproducing some of their most famous wines like Soave, Valpolicella and Chianti — which happened as soon as they saw they could be sold in bulk abroad — and started to lower their standards of production. Fortunately much of what stays at home is perfectly drinkable. The Italians aren't stupid enough to let their best wines leave the country!

There is, however, some government control over wine production. Until about 20 years ago anyone could make anything and call it what he liked. Most wine was made by private vineyard owners and sold by dealers who poured it into strange shaped bottles that found their way onto the tables of hotels and restaurants. If you got a good one you were lucky.

Politically Italian wine is difficult to control, but recently the government has started to make quality controls more stringent. These days there's still a lot of plonk around but Italy also produces some of the best wine in the world. In the past, some of the Chianti that turned up on restaurant tables and supermarket shelves was dreadful, but a new law states that any wine produced since 1984 has now to conform to the DOCG status (see p. 101). This means in practice that any 'young' Chianti you buy should be perfectly good. A wine like Lambrusco is a bit more difficult to control, since it's made in a region that politically is less inclined to respond to government regulations. But Lambrusco, which can be sweet and quite nasty abroad, is very different in Italy. The local variety is dry, not sweet, and it is made to complement the local food dishes of the region. Because that's what it is all about. Wine and food are produced to taste good together, and just as the food varies from region to region, so too does the wine. Within Italy wines don't travel around very much, so while you may see a red Cannonau in Sardinia you probably won't see it in the Veneto. Drink what the locals do and you won't go far wrong.

Many of the most prolific wine producing areas have clearly marked wine routes to follow if you've got a car, particularly Tuscany, Piedmont and the Veneto. Look for signs saying *Strada del Vino* and they'll lead you not only past vineyards but also to *enoteche* where you can stop and do some serious tasting, and buying if you want to.

So, when you're contemplating a wine to go with your meal don't go for the names you already know from your supermarket shelves back home but look for something local and different. Experiment, ask locally for advice and the chances are you'll discover something special.

CLASSIC WINES

There are a handful of wines in Italy that are virtually house-hold names. On their home territory they may be very different from the versions that are exported. If you see the word *classico* after the name, it means the wine is the best, in that it comes from the heart of the area of production:

Bardolino (Veneto) Red

Bardolino is a pale red with an almost rose shimmering light that some people say reflects the water of Lake Garda on whose hillsides the grapes grow. It has a delicate bouquet and is slightly fruity. Choose a young wine (no more than a year old) and look for producers like Ca Furia, Colle dei Cipressi, Fratelli Poggi, Girasole, Lamberti Le Tende and Santi.

Chianti (Tuscany) Red

Chianti is the name of a huge family of wines with a number of rich and poor relations. Chianti is a blend of grapes, mostly red with a small proportion of white, blended to a formula devised in the nineteenth century. Since 1984 standards have been raised considerably, so the young wines are reliably of better quality. They have to conform to the DOCG status. The best are labelled as *classico* or *riserva* which means that the wine has been aged for a minimum of three years. Also look for the seal of a black cockerel on the neck of the bottle. One of the best is Chianti Ruffino Riserva Ducale.

Lambrusco (Emilia Romagna) Red or White

Lambrusco is the most popular wine in the world, selling annually over 132 million bottles. Twenty years ago it was never seen abroad but an enterprising wine producer decided to try and market it outside Italy by reducing its alcohol content to little more than beer, and sweetening it considerably. The resulting sweet, slightly fizzy wine took off like a rocket and today lines supermarket shelves the world over. In Emilia Romagna the Lambrusco you can buy is the original version, an excellent, dry, slightly tart wine produced to complement the region's cuisine. It bears no resemblance whatsoever to the exported variety.

Orvieto (Umbria and Latium) White

Orvieto may be a best seller but it is nothing very special. Its vineyards have been grossly exploited and overproduced: the result either a dry (labelled *secco* on the bottle) almost neutral wine that will go with most things if you're thirsty enough, or the rather more individual sweet or *abboccato* version. The best, the Classico comes from the vines nearest to the town of Orvieto itself, and it will have a DOC status after its name.

Soave (Veneto) White

Soave from Verona ranks second only to Chianti in importance as a DOC wine. It is a refreshing, versatile, dry white wine that goes well with any summertime meal. The best wines are produced around the town of Soave — the Classico — which is slightly stronger than the ordinary Soave. Drink it young and choose wines from a well-known producer like Bolla or Bertani.

Valpolicella (Veneto) Red

You can recognise a Valpolicella by its rich almost luminous ruby red colour. It smells fruity and is best drunk young. It may be chilled. It comes from the vineyards around Verona and Lake Garda and, like Chianti, it is well travelled, with the exported version having a lot less character. Look for wines produced by Allegrini, Bolla, Le Ragose, Giuseppe Quintarelli, Sanperetto and Tedeschi.

Verdicchio (Marches) White

Verdicchio is instantly recognisable by its slim green amphora-shaped bottle. You'll see them on virtually every restaurant table along the Adriatic (although other producers produce it in ordinary bottles). The wine is straw coloured and it has a delicate smell and a full robust body that goes well with fish dishes. It takes its name from the greenish yellow grape it's made from. There are two sorts: along the coast you'll mostly see the Castelli di Jesi, inland the Matelica which is fuller, heavier and has a higher alcohol content. Good producers are Fazi-Brunori (who designed the bottle) and M. Brunori.

THE DIFFERENT REGIONS

The biggest wine producing regions are Emilia Romagna, Apulia, Sicily, the Veneto and Piedmont, in that order. The north produces better quality wines than the south and the bulk of DOC wines are from northern vineyards.

Mountains seem to play an important part in protecting

the grape from adverse climatic conditions. The Alps shield the vines from the damp of central Europe and the Apennines play a large part in controlling the weather from Piedmont right down to Calabria. Even Sicily has her own Mount Etna to protect her vines.

The cooler climate of the north benefits the grape by allowing a slow ripening season that concentrates the flavour and doesn't allow the grapes to overcrop or become too sweet. Imported varieties like Cabernet, Pinot Noir, Chardonnay, Riesling and Sauvignon grow quite happily alongside native varieties. Italy's major wine schools are also in the north and they are largely responsible for the high standards of many of the wines produced in this area.

There are literally thousands of different wines to choose from. If you are really serious about buying or trying some of the more unusual wines you will need to take with you a good wine guidebook to Italy. I can highly recommend Victor Hazan's *Italian Wine* (Penguin), although it is thick and quite heavy for travelling, or Nicolas Belfrage's *Life Beyond Lambrusco — Understanding Italian Fine Wine* (Sidgwick & Jackson).

I've grouped wines very roughly into regions so you can see what you could or should be drinking depending on which part of Italy you are visiting.

Wines of Northern Italy

Piedmont, which means 'at the foot of the mountain' is the region bordering France and Switzerland and it produces two of the best red wines in all Italy; Barolo and Barbaresco, both from the *nebbiolo* grape. Some say that Barolo is one of the best reds in the world. It should be drunk at least three years old (four years for a *riserva*). It has a memorable 'nose' and flavour. Keep the bottle upright for some time before you plan to drink it and pour it very gently because there is likely to be sediment at the bottom of the bottle. Alternatively you can pour the wine very carefully into a decanter, stopping before you get to the sediment. Barbaresco is similar to Barolo but slightly drier.

Also worth seeking out among red wines are: Gattinara, Grignolino, Spanna (a local name for the *nebbiolo* grape), Barbera d'Alba and Dolcetto which although red can be slightly 'prickly', or a full blown *frizzante* or sparkling wine.

Piedmont is also well known for its sweet sparkling white wines made from the Moscato grape. Asti Spumante (which means fizzy) is an excellent wine to drink young and fresh. It is also very cheap in Italy. Moscato d'Asti is much the same thing, but is made outside the tightly controlled Asti Spumante area. This can be very low in alcohol – a good 'family' wine. As well as its wines Piedmont also produces a wide range of Italian vermouths (see p. 109).

Emilia Romagna produces Lambrusco, which in Italy is very different from the exported version (see p. 101). The Ligurian Riviera doesn't produce much of note but it's worth trying Vermentino, fresh, smooth or white or trying to find the rare, sweet, dry white Cinqueterre. The red berrylike Rossere di Dolceacqua is the best red in the area.

In the north-east they produce more wines for export than anywhere else in the country including the Veneto's famous reds; Valpolicella and Bardolino and the white Soave. Try too the Veneto's white Gambellara DOC. In the Alto Adige and Trentino try the Pinot Grigo, north of Venice in Conegliano they produce an excellent dry white sparkling wine called Prosecco di Conegliano, in Friuli on the border with Yugoslavia try the white Tocai del Collio. In the Dolomites, which border Austria, the wines are often compared to those of Alsace and include a number of high quality including the white Chardonnay.

A number of dessert wines are also good including the Recioto della Valpolicella and Torcolato from the Veneto which you'll find if you're holidaying along the Adriatic coast near Venice or, further towards Trieste, Friuli's Ramandolo.

Wines of Central Italy

Central Italy is responsible for some of Italy's best and worst wines. Above all it is known for its Chianti from Tuscany, Orvieto from Umbria, Latium's Frascati, and Verdicchio from the Marches (see p. 102). Up behind the Adriatic beaches in the Marches behind Ancona, you'll find vineyards that produce good wines like the Rosso Piceno DOC and Rosso Conero. In Tuscany as well as Chianti Classico try: the red Carmignano Riserva and the Vino Nobile di Montepulciano (named after the grape and the town), the white Galestra and Vin Santo as a dessert wine. The Abruzzi makes little quality or DOC wine – much will be local plonk. Look out for the red Montepulciano d'Abruzzo and the white Trebbiano d'Abruzzo for something a bit better than average. Latium (with Rome as its centre) is a prolific wine region with the vines growing in the Roman hills. The white Frascati and Orvieto are, of course, the most famous (see p. 101) but there are numerous other wines, like Est! Est! Est! If you've got a car, it is well worth doing a tour of the *castelli Romani*

(Roman castles) and visiting wine producing towns like Velletri and the Colli Albani, calling in at simple *frasca* (bar with a laurel wreath above the doorway) for a glass or two.

Wines of Southern Italy

The south is known for making vast quantities of ordinary quality wine. The vines grow in the volcanic soil of vineyards on the mountain slopes well above sea level and in the gently rolling countryside. There are numerous different wine varieties most of which you'll only see locally but there are a number of wines well worth singling out as follows.

The island of Ischia produced the very first DOC wine in 1966, but it is the larger island of Sicily where you'll make the best discoveries.

In Sicily, Etna's own DOC wine (red, white or rose) is produced from the fertile volcanic soil on her slopes, try too the red Corvo Rosso and white Corvo Bianco. The best wines of the region have a Q on the bottle denoting quality. Sicily is well known too for its production of the sweet dessert wine Marsala which is fermented in great vats (you can smell it as soon as you approach the town) on the west coast of the island. Bottles stamped *vergine* are the best. Try too the dry Vecchio Samperi as an aperitif.

If you should be staying on the Aeolian Islands north of Sicily (you can visit them for a day from Milazzo or Cefalu), Lipari produces a Malvasia sweet dessert wine which is regarded as one of the best in Italy.

If you are holidaying along the Neapolitan Riviera (Campania) you will have a wide choice of wines. Look for a 'big' red called Taurasi which comes from the Campanian hills near Avellino which a lot of people rate as highly as Barolo, and for a Taurasi Riserva from Mastroberardino for something really special. Of the whites the most famous is Lacryma Christi (the tears of Christ), try too Greco and the dry Fiano di Avellino.

On the east coast (around Bari), Apulia produces an excellent Favonio, Torre Quartro and Rosa del Golfo.

In Calabria, in the far south, one of the best wines is the red Ciro and the Greco di Bianco makes a pleasant sweet aperitif.

Sardinia's white grapes are totally different from any others and many of her wines have a high alcoholic content, so be warned. Try Vermentino with fish or as an aperitif or the Malvasia di Cagliari DOC. For a sweet wine (as a *liquoroso* or a dessert wine) try one of the several Moscato wines. Of the reds the Cannonau is well worth singling out.

WHAT TO LOOK FOR – ON THE BOTTLE

There are ways of making sure you find a quality wine. Roughly 10 per cent of all wine is considered good enough to be awarded the DOC status. DOC means *Denominazione di Origine Controllata* and is the official classification of a quality wine, given by an expert committee of the Italian Department of Agriculture which supervises the suitability of vineyards as well as growers and producers, and authorises the issue of labels. The DOC mark means that the producer has had to prove that the production of grapes from his vineyard is limited to a set minimum, the wine produced has a minimum alcohol content and the quantity of 'must' or juice obtained from the grape during pressing does not exceed an agreed level. In many cases there is also an agreed period of minimum ageing so that the wine cannot be sold until it has reached an acceptable level of maturation. DOC status implies the wine is 'typical' of its type. The wines do not have to be submitted to taste tests though, so the status is not infallible.

Of Italy's many thousands of wines about 220 are good enough to qualify for the DOC status. You're very unlikely to see the words DOC on a bottle that is 'capped' rather than 'corked'.

Classico after the name means that the wine was produced in the heart of the wine-producing area. It is applied to the best wines so, for example, a Chianti Classico will be infinitely superior to a plain Chianti.

DOCG stands for *Denominazione di Origine Controllata e Garantita*. This status is reserved for even better quality wines and its numbers are strictly limited. When a type of wine moves up from being DOC to DOCG every producer has to submit samples for tasting. A welcome addition to the DOCG status is Chianti where standards of production were seriously declining. All Chianti bottled after 1984 has to conform to the DOCG standards. The same applies to the Vino Nobile di Montepulciano, Barolo and Barbaresco from Piedmont. You may pay a bit more but you'll know what you're getting.

Vino da Tavola is the name given to ordinary table wines. This doesn't mean to say though that they aren't any good. They may be excellent – occasionally even better than a DOC wine. The reason is that there are plenty of growers who don't want to become involved in registering their vineyards and being assessed for a designated appellation. They prefer to just get on with it in their own way. Growers who use grapes not approved in their particular area, 'classic' varieties from elsewhere such as Cabernet Sauvignon, can't get a classification either and some of these wines can be excellent, like the Pinot Blanc, for example, of Apulia. In general, *vino da tavola* is nothing to write home about. What makes Italian wines so exciting though is that lurking in among the ordinary are bottles of outstanding merit.

The Bottle

A bottle of wine can contain a bewildering amount of information. Starting from the top:

The Seal. This often has a label on it indicating that the producer belongs to a growers' consortium. It is a voluntary association which monitors quality levels and fosters wine production to standards above the legal minimum. The emblem is not necessarily a guarantee of quality. For example, the consortium who are responsible for the Chianti Classico mark their seal with a black cockerel.

The Year. This is obviously important as there are good and bad vintages even within regions. The age is important too because it tells you what stage of development the wine has reached and whether it is at its best for drinking. This means you actually have to know when to drink a particular wine or when the best year was.

The Name. Italians do not follow conventions when it comes to naming their wines. They may call it after the grape, the vineyard or area, or even the producer's wife. To make things even more confusing the same name might apply to both red and white wines. The better the wine is the more likely it is to be called after the area of cultivation. Where there are two names, like Brunello di Montcalcino, the first name is the main grape and the second is the area in which it is produced.

Producer's Name. This is very important. The best Italian wines are made by a handful of producers (one of whom is Bolla). If you recognise a good name you can be pretty sure the wine is of a good quality.

Country of Origin. Of course this should be Italy. 'Bottled in area of origin' guarantees that the wine has been bottled in the area it was cultivated in (*imbottigliato nella zona di produzione*), and is a guarantee that you are actually drinking what you think you are.

Bottom Line. This isn't terribly important; it covers the contents following EEC guidelines. Then comes the official control number of the bottler and then the alcohol content.

GLOSSARY OF WINE TERMS

Abboccato	Mild, sweet wine
Acidita	Acidity
Alcool	Alcohol
Amaro	Bitter
Amabile	Medium sweet
Bianco	White
Cantina	Wine cellar
Cantina sociale	Wine co-operative
Chiaretto	Rosé from red grape
Contenuto	Contents
Co-operatia viticola	Wine-producing co-operative
Delicato	Light and soft
Dolce	Sweet
Fattoria	Wine-growing estate
Fiasco	Flask
Frizzante	Semi-sparkling
Fruttate	Fruity
Grado alcolico	Alcohol content
Invecchiato	Stored, matured
Leggero	Light
Liquoroso	High alcohol
Morbido	Soft
Pieno	Full bodied
Profumato	Strong bouquet
Riserva	Wine that has had the benefit of more maturing time
Rosato	Rosé
Rosso	Red
Secco	Dry
Semi secco	Medium sweet
Spumante	Sparkling
Superiore	Higher than minimum strength. Could be better quality
Tenuta	Vineyard
Uve	Grapes

Vecchio	Old wine, indicating one or two years ageing beyond legal minimum, usually less than *riserva*
Vite	Vine
Viticoltore	Wine grower
Viticoltura	Wine growing

SPIRITS

Aperitivi and *Digestivi*

Italians drink their before and after dinner drinks, not at the table but generally at a bar. In the summer everyone spends a lot of time out of doors and wherever you are in Italy, at about six or seven in the evening you'll see Italians walking up and down the main street, arms linked, taking their daily *passegiata*. When they get tired of this they'll either stand at the bar or, if they want to linger, sit down at a pavement table and have an aperitif. After dinner they may have their digestif in the restaurant but most likely they'll head off to the bars again. In your own villa or apartment there's nothing nicer than lingering over a summertime drink, particularly if you've got a garden or balcony.

There will be a lot of Italian drinks that you are probably already familiar with. Vermouth is produced in Piedmont in Turin, manufactured by blending extracts of aromatic plants with, originally, the Moscato grape, but increasingly with wines from Sicily and southern Italy. Both Martini e Rossi and Cinzano are available in *bianco* (white) and *rosso* (red), both sweet. Martini have also added a *rosato* (rosé). The dry white is labelled *secco*. You'll probably also know Campari which is made from herbs, the peel of bitter oranges and quinine bark steeped in spirits. Try drinking it with white wine. As for the rest, look behind any bar and you'll see literally hundreds of unfamiliar looking bottles. Try a few. The glossary below might help identify some of them.

Amaretto A rich golden-coloured liqueur made from the kernels of apricot stones. Very sweet. Amaro is a well-known brand. Mixed with a little butter and spread on a cooked crêpe you can then refry it and you'll have a delicious tasting sauce.

Aperol A non-alcoholic bitter.

Aurum Citrus-flavoured liqueur.

Centerbe Also known as Mentuccia, minty flavoured liqueur, said to be a blend of a hundred herbs.

Cynar A bitter sweet drink made from the essence of artichokes, it is drunk with soda and lemon as an aperitif, or neat as a digestif. Said to work wonders if you have trouble with your gall bladder.

Fernet Branca A bitter, highly herby, faintly medicinal drink that, say the Italians, cures all ills. It would have to, no-one would drink it for fun. The *Menta* variety is an attempt to make it more palatable.

Fior d'Alpi Herb liqueur made of alpine herbs and flowers.

Galliano Another herb liqueur, you'll recognise the distinctive, tall conical bottle. Named after a war hero whose picture often appears on the label. Used in cocktails.

Grappa Every country has its equivalent of fire water. This is Italy's, made from the distillation of the stalks and pips. Overdosing guarantees a hangover.

Latte di Suocera Literally, mother in law's milk, a sweet, herb-flavoured liqueur.

Maraschino Originally from the coast which is now part of Yugoslavia, but now made in Italy, a colourless cherry brandy.

Millefiori A sweet herb liqueur made from the essence of a 'thousand' flowers.

Pelinkovac A bitter sweet dark liqueur based on herbs and red wine.

Punt e Mes Dark red, a bit like Dubonnet.

Sambucca Colourless liqueur that tastes like aniseed, served *con mosche* with 'flies', coffee beans floating on the surface, roasted or flambéed as they are brought to your table.

Stock Italian brand of brandy.

Strega Herbs soaked in spirit, rather like Benedictine; the word means witch and a man and a woman who drink it together are meant to be united for ever.

13

CHILDREN AND THOSE ON SPECIAL DIETS

CHILDREN

Babies, toddlers and fussy children who tend to be suspicious of foreign food won't have much to complain about in Italy. I've yet to meet a child of any age who isn't happy on a diet of spaghetti, pizza and home-made ice-cream — which makes life pretty simple in Italy as that's what's available.

For babies you can get a wide range of jars and packets of food in supermarkets, *alimentari* or *farmacia*. However while you may find familiar brands (like Gerber and Milupa) you will see that Italian babies eat Plasmon, Heinz jars manufactured under the Plasmon label, though some varieties will be different. Nipiol Buitoni produce a *sensa glutine* range — without gluten. You could try Plasmon's tiny *micron* pasta shapes or *astrini* (stars), fruit purées (*albicocche mediterranee* might make a change) and meat dishes. While you're eating your *saltimboca alla romana* try your baby on *omogeniezzato vitello* in a jar! You can buy *semolino* (semolina) for pudding or as a rice cereal, *crema di riso*, to both you just add milk or water. Although you can get Milupa you may not find the flavours your baby is used to. If in doubt pack a few packets to make up when you arrive.

There is no need at all to pack disposable nappies. There are ample supplies everywhere: in clothes shops, *farmacia*, *alimentari* and supermarkets. And you can buy a wide range of clothes, sunhats and toys.

Remember that if you haven't been able to boil tap water for at least ten minutes or sterilised it with water sterilising tablets, you should use mineral water to reconstitute packets.

If your child is drinking real milk, *scremato* is skimmed; *parzialmente scremato*, semi-skimmed; *pastorizzato*, normal pasteurised milk; *intero*, rather rich full cream milk. Powdered varieties are, of course, available everywhere, but brands may not be the ones your baby is familiar with, so take your own with you.

Italian teething babies are given *crosta di pane* (bread-crusts), carrots or a wedge of *parmigiano* to gnaw on.

So much for babies. Young children in Italy get quickly used to slices of salami (not actually very good for them as they contain preservatives and too much salt), wedges of watermelon, even little olives and artichoke hearts in jars of oil that you find in the *alimentari*! Most toddlers will eat pasta and their mums cut up 'real' food small for them. A teatime treat is a bowl of *mascarpone* (a thick creamy cheese) whipped up with an egg yolk and a little sugar. In summer when *mascarpone* may not be around as it goes off quickly you can buy it in tins (Galbani do it). Try spreading *Nutella* (chocolate and hazelnut spread) on some bread. The local *pannetiere* will sell squares of *focaccia*, a bread either plain or baked with olive oil and salt. You can also get it with cheese, onions or with sage and olives for older children. The plain ones can be filled with ham or cheese. *Pane toscano* is also popular with children. Simply toast a piece of bread onto which you've squashed a tomato! There are also plenty of varieties of yoghurt to try. And cartons of juice.

SPECIAL DIETS

Anyone on a low fat diet should find *ricotta* a versatile cheese (it's mostly water). You can serve it mixed with fruit, cinnamon or vegetables. You'll find so much fresh fruit and interesting salad that dieting is a pleasure in Italy.

Diabetics should find that supermarkets and *farmacia* have some sugarfree jams, biscuits and chocolates. There are often local clinics for diabetics should you run into difficulties. You can also buy sugarfree drinks in *farmacia*.

If you are on a high fibre diet you can usually find wholemeal bread (*pane integrale*) and wholemeal pasta, in restaurants and in supermarkets and, of course, there are plenty of fresh vegetables. The following words might help:

Artificial sweetener	*Dolcificante*
Caffein-free	*Decaffeinato*
Do you have … for diabetics	*Avete … per diabetici*
Do you have vegetarian dishes	*Avete dei piatti vegetariani*
Flour/Fat	*Farina/Grasso*
I'm on a diet	*Sono a dieta*

CHILDREN AND THOSE ON SPECIAL DIETS

I mustn't eat food containing *Non devo mangiare cibi che
contengono ...*
Salt/Sugar *Sale/Zucchero*

14
EATING AND DRINKING OUT

So convinced are the Italians of the excellence of their cooking that you'd be hard pressed to find food of another nationality.

Italians eat dinner (*la cena*) late (seldom before 8.00 p.m.), especially the further south you go. They have their main meal at lunchtime (*il pranzo* — between 12.30 and 2.30 or 3.00 p.m.), and Sunday is when the whole family eats out together — everyone from great grandpa who tends to hold forth with his serviette tucked firmly under his chin at the end of the table, to toddlers who spend most of the meal tucking into the pasta.

Italians love children and welcome them. The waiters will more than likely whisk them away into the kitchen where they may stay for a while, emerging with their faces covered in (free) ice-cream.

Get to know the manager or owner as soon as you arrive, tell him you want to try his specialities (*specialità della casa*) and, if you're lucky and he's not too busy, you'll get all sorts of things to sample before you order.

TYPES OF RESTAURANT

Smaller places, *trattoria* or, in the country *osteria* (inns), or *locanda* (a simple place serving local dishes) are usually family run, with grandma at the till taking the money and the rest of the family in and out of the kitchen. You probably won't be offered a menu (there may be one but it won't be worth bothering with). The dishes will be freshly prepared that morning — *casalinga* (home cooking) rather than elaborate dishes — perhaps a few specialities of the day, probably a soup and a pasta dish, good local bread, a roast meat or fish, a vegetable or two and cheese or fruit. Sounds boring? It won't be. The waiter will tell you what's cooking or you can just look around at what other people are eating and point. Don't avoid a restaurant just because it doesn't look as if it has much to offer. The food will usually be a lot better than in a bigger town restaurant that actually sticks to standard dishes on a menu. Do ask about payment though before you tuck in. Some out of the way places have never seen traveller's cheques, and won't accept credit cards, though I've managed with foreign currency using the newspaper's exchange rate.

A *ristorante*, will be altogether more formal. The menu will be larger and you'll get a better choice of food and wine. It will be more expensive.

Follow the crowds. The Italians know where to go. Never go into a restaurant that's empty (although early lunchtimes or evenings may be quiet).

Cover charge (*coperto*) is shown separately and service is added automatically to the end of the bill. You should leave the small change (a couple of hundred lire) as a tip. You must, by law, take away your *ricevuta fiscale* (receipt) with you, you can be fined outside the restaurant if you can't produce it.

THE MENU

Some restaurants have a fixed tourist menu — *menu a prezzo fisso*. It will usually be good value.

The first course is an *antipasto* or *hors d'oeuvre*. In a restaurant these will be set out on a table. In a smaller place a plate of *antipasto assortito* will just arrive! A likely *antipasto* will be a plateful of local hams or *salame*, perhaps Parma ham with melon or figs, *mozzarella* with tomato, asparagus, a plate of beans with olive oil, mixed vegetables or salads, perhaps little shrimps gently fried or *calamari* (squid).

Next come the *minestre* (soups, rice or pasta) as a *primo*. Italians are quite keen on soups, from thick vegetable *minestrone* to thin *consommé*. You'll get risotto dishes in the north and a choice of pasta dishes. Some will be easy to identify, some won't as they may be named after anyone from the owner's wife to a famous guest who happened to be passing through.

The *secondi piatti* or main course may be headed *piatti del giorno* (dishes of the day), or simply divided into *pesce* or *carne* (fish or meat). Anywhere along the coast will produce vast platters of *fritto misto* (mixed fried fish), platefuls of mussels, fried rings of squid, large crayfish or a whole roast fish sprinkled with herbs.

The meat may be veal escalopes (*scaloppine*), much may be *arrosto* (roasted), look out for the tender *bistecca alla Fiorentina* — sold by the kilo.

Vegetables (*legumi*, *verdure* or *contorni*) may accompany the main course or may be served on their own. Do not expect them to be piping hot, some dishes are served tepid or even cold. Vegetables are seldom just simply boiled, they may be seasoned, *farciti* (stuffed) or fried in batter. *Legumi di stagione* will be a selection of the season's vegetables.

Formaggi (cheese) won't be an elaborate cheese board but a selection of local cheeses, often made with sheep or goat's milk. *Frutta* (fruit) may be fresh or *macedonia* (fruit salad).

Gelati (ice-cream) may be frozen into cakes and perhaps decorated with nuts.

Dolce is a selection of *pasticceria* (cakes). Desserts don't take up much room on menus; the waiter will usually tell you what he has.

SNACKS

There are many places to have something quick to eat or drink:

Gelateria sell ice-cream, all sorts, in cornets, in cups (*coppa*), in dishes or in tall glasses. Most are meals in themselves. You may or not be able to sit down.

Paninoteca are a fairly new innovation, a sort of coffee shop/sandwich bar where you can buy filled rolls (*panini*), and sandwiches, toasted or otherwise.

Pizzeria are often only open in the evening. They usually have a large oven and bake the pizzas there in front of you. Numerous toppings, a cheap way of eating out.

Rosticceria specialise in roast and grilled meats, often marinated in herbs first. You can often sit down rather than just takeaway and you may also get pasta dishes like *lasagne*.

Tavola calda are self-service restaurants where you can get a hot meal. You may have to eat standing up but there will be a good choice of freshly made dishes.

DRINKING OUT

Bars Italians make good use of their bars; they open in time for breakfast (and do a roaring trade in stand up *espressos*, *brioche* and sandwiches — *panini imbottiti.*) Most bars close well after midnight. They all sell alcoholic drinks as well as tea, coffee, hot chocolate, fruit drinks and, of course, ice-cream. The shelves at the back will be full of *aperitivi* and *digestivi* bottles — many of which you won't see outside Italy. Or you can just drink wine.

Prices double as soon as you sit down. It's the price you pay for service and taking the weight off your feet, and there are many bars all over Italy well worth sitting down for, like those in St Mark's Square in Venice. In summer most bars have tables outside on the pavement and you can while away a good few hours before and after dinner watching the world go by. If you do decide to stand up you have to pay the cashier first by telling him what you want and then hand the ticket over in exchange for your food or drink.

Bars also do a roaring trade in giving directions, providing loos and telling people where the nearest phone is if they haven't got one.

Caffè (Coffee Shop) Coffee was first tasted in Italy in 1640 — as a medicine! It was sold in pharmacies. The first cafe opened in Venice 40 years later and others quickly followed. A *caffè* quickly became more than just a place to drink coffee — it was a meeting place for artists, politicians, revolutionaries and socialites. Men would entertain in their favourite *caffé* rather than at home; newspapers were available on long poles and the decor was as elegant as any drawing room. Several Italian *caffés* are still as they have been for centuries: the Caffè Greco in Rome, Florian in Venice and the Caffè Pedrocchi in Padua are just three. On a recent visit to Padua, a student with a laurel wreath round her neck (she had just passed her exams) was holding a party in the Pedrocchi — and passing round delicate truffle sandwiches! Most cafes serve cakes, pastries, *brioche* and drinks, including alcohol. They also do a brisk trade in breakfasts.

Glossary of Drinking in Bars and Cafes

Aperitif	*Un aperitivo*
A beer	*Una birra*
A bottle	*Una bottiglia*
Double	*Doppio*
Drinks	*Bevande*
A glass	*Un bicchiere*
Neat	*Liscio*
On the rocks	*Con ghiaccio*
With water	*Con acqua*
Wine	*Vino*

Beer

You can buy beer in bars, restaurants and in supermarkets. The Italian brands aren't as strong as ours.

Bottled	*In bottiglia*
Draught	*Alla spina*
Foreign	*Straniera, estera*
Italian	*Nazionale*
Light	*Bionda, chiara*
Dark	*Scura*

Non-Alcoholic Drinks

Espresso is drunk all over Italy at all times of day. Italians drink it strong and black. If you want it diluted ask for *alto* or *lungo*, or with a splash of milk, *macchiato*. At breakfast they drink *cappuccino*, a frothy cup of coffee with hot milk and a sprinkling of chocolate on the top. At night they add a shot of grappa or other strong liqueur; ask for it *corretto*. Iced coffees don't really exist. A *caffè freddo* will be a thick, sweet drink served cold but not iced and *tè freddo* will be cold and pre-sweetened. Camomile tea is also popular.

Hot chocolate is always popular with children. It is usually served in a teapot and is often so strong you can almost stand your spoon up in it. For children it is quite difficult to get hold of a straight orange squash. The alternatives are fizzy orange or coke. Freshly-squeezed orange in summer goes down well with most children but it can be expensive especially if you sit down at a cafe. The bottled *succhi di frutta* are delicious (flavours are pear, peach, apple and orange) but they are very sweet. Try a milkshake (*frappé*) with ice-cream or a fruitshake (*frullati*), fresh fruit and sometimes milk blended together. A *granita* is a sort of Italian slushpuppy, a sorbet made of crushed ice that's virtually drinkable. You can get it in a glass with a blob of whipped cream on top. In summer ask for a *granita con fragole con panna* (iced crushed strawberries with cream).

GLOSSARY OF EATING AND DRINKING OUT

The bill	*Il conto*
Could we have a table?	*Potremmo avere un tavolo?*
(outside)	(*all'aperto*)
May I have the menu?	*Posso avere il menu?*
Waiter	*Cameriere*
Waitress	*Cameriera*
What do you recommend?	*Cosa consiglia?*

WORDS – IN RESTAURANTS

Baked, grilled	*Al forno, al ferri*
Bread	*Pane*
Butter	*Burro*
Cheese	*Formaggio*
Dish of the day	*Piatto del giorno*
Extra charge	*Supplemento*
First course	*Primo*
Fish course	*Pesce*
Grilled	*Alla griglia*
Meat course	*Carne*
Oil	*Olio*
On skewers	*Allo spiedo*
Pepper	*Pepe*
Roast	*Arrosto*
Salt	*Sale*
Second course	*Secondo*
Smoked	*Affumicato*
Speciality of the house	*Specialita della casa*
Stewed	*In umido*
Sugar	*Zucchero*
Sweets	*Dolci*
Vegetables	*Contorni*
Vinegar	*Aceto*

SNACK WORDS

Chips	*Patatine fritte*
Chocolate bar	*Stecca di cioccolata*
Chicken (half)	*Pollo (meta)*
Rolls	*Panini*
Sandwich	*Panino imbottito*
cheese	*formaggio*
ham (cooked)	*prosciutto cotto*
ham (raw)	*prosciutto crudo*
salami	*salame*
Slice of pizza	*Fetta di pizza*

GLOSSARY OF NON-ALCOHOLIC DRINKS

Chocolate (hot)	*Cioccolata calda*
with cream	*con panna*
Coffee (small black cup)	*Espresso*

Coffee (black)	*Caffè nero*
Coffee (diluted)	*Alto, lungo*
Coffee (white)	*Caffè latte*
(splash of milk)	*caffè macchiato*
(with hot milk and cocoa)	*cappuccino*
Coffee (with liqueur)	*Corretto*
Crushed sorbet/ice	*Granita*
Fizzy	*Gassata, spumante*
Freshly squeezed lemon	*Spremuta di limone*
Freshly squeezed orange	*Spremuta d'arancia*
Fruit juice	*Succo di frutta*
Fruitshake	*Frullato di frutta*
Iced tea	*Tè freddo*
Lemonade	*Limonata*
Milk	*Latte*
Milkshake	*Frappé*
Mineral water	*Acqua minerale*
Orangeade	*Aranciata*
Non-carbonated	*Naturale*
Tea	*Tè*
Tea with lemon	*Tè con limone*
Tomato juice	*Succo di pomodoro*

15

WHAT TO TAKE WITH YOU

I once witnessed an English family arrive at the villa they'd rented in Tuscany with their car boot packed full of tins of baked beans, sacks of potatoes, saucepans, tin openers, tin foil and toilet rolls. Nowhere in Italy is that remote!

Although you probably won't know exactly what's going to be in your holiday home you can be sure that your kitchen will be adequately supplied with pots and pans and that the shop around the corner will stock almost everything else you're likely to need.

It is tempting on a self-catering holiday, even in this country, to take all sorts of unnecessary things. But you should think twice. Not only is it fun to be versatile and make do with what you find but, unless you're travelling with very young children or anyone on a special diet, buying locally should be part of the enjoyment of the holiday!

There are plenty of dishes you can make, even if all you've got are a couple of wooden spoons and a frying pan. You may have to adapt recipes, as some holiday rentals only run to a hob or hotplate rather than a grill or an oven. The hobs may be gas (cylinder) or electric. Fortunately Italians do a lot of cooking on the top so you shouldn't be short of recipes. You are unlikely to find a food processor or a blender provided, but you'll probably find a colander and sieve, and a large saucepan for cooking pasta. Another thing to bear in mind is that you'll probably have to get used to boiling water in a saucepan (kettles are rare), and while you may get a rolling pin you may not be provided with an eggcup, so pack both if they are important to you. Don't expect too much and you may be pleasantly surprised at what you find lurking in the back of a drawer.

If you're renting through a tour operator or even privately

there are certain things you should try to find out in advance, for example, whether linen is provided and whether you get a 'welcome' pack on arrival. There's nothing worse than arriving when all the shops are shut to find the cupboards are bare!

Welcome packs usually consist of a couple of teabags, small containers of jam, perhaps milk and bread, a few eggs and sugar — enough for your first breakfast. If you know you aren't going to get one it is worth either stopping off for a few groceries on the way or packing a small box of staples to start you off.

Most apartments or villas look desperately empty on arrival. If you're lucky there will be some toilet paper, washing up liquid, cleaner for the bath and a few cloths, but don't bank on it.

When visiting to Italy for a short holiday, say a week, I've always found it rather a waste of money buying large quantities of things like sugar, salt, teabags, cooking oil, washing up liquid, J-cloths, etc. when I arrive. They all seem to come in huge packs which one barely uses and ends up leaving for the next occupants. If you can, get hold of some plastic bottles from the chemist, you can decant essentials (label them clearly) and take small supplies with you (they are actually also quite useful for picnics). Don't overdo it though; limit yourself to as much as you can pack into a small box. Obviously if you are travelling by air, it isn't going to be very practical to take much with you.

Travelling with small children and babies involves a bit more thought. It is important to take their own cups, plastic spoons and bowls. A thermos flask is essential too (for keeping boiled water to make up packets or milk, and for carrying cold drinks down to the beach). I always used to take a *mouli* too (food grinder) when my daughter was small — puréed, she'd eat anything. And I've found it useful to make sauces too.

There are only a few things you can't get, or are much more expensive in Italy, that you might consider taking with you. Orange squash is virtually unheard of. Coffee is very expensive and, although you can get breakfast cereals, familiar brands are expensive.

As for things for the kitchen, the local market will have a hardware stall where you can pick up things like fluted pastry wheels for cutting pasta, or a corkscrew should your villa not have one.

WHAT TO TAKE WITH YOU

Here's a list of things I've found most useful to take with me rather than to have to start looking for when I arrive:

bottle opener/corkscrew
candles
clingfilm/plastic wrap
clothes pegs
garlic press
good sharp knife
grater (Parmesan and nutmeg)
matches
plastic bags (picnics, leftovers)
potato peeler
silverfoil
string (washing and asparagus bundles)
teabags
teatowels and J-cloths
thermos flask
tin opener
torch/flashlight
wire whisk
and (non essential but worth a thought):
melon scoop (for removing pulp for stuffed tomatoes and for melon or ice-cream)
peppermill (if you can't do without)
a three-footed ring to put in the bottom of a pan to convert it to a *bain marie*

16
RECIPES

These recipes are for four people unless otherwise stated.
They are mostly fairly simple. Your equipment may be rather
limited so you may have to be adaptable. Your holiday
kitchen may have a grill or an oven but may not have both;
some only have hobs or hotplates. As for pots and pans, you
will have to make do with what you find. A lot of the recipes
involve adding water, in Italy make sure it is from a bottle,
not the tap.

All weights and measures are given in the local metric
equivalents as well as pounds and ounces. A table of weights
and measures is given at the end of the book for reference.

Bear in mind that most Italians couldn't tell you the exact
ingredients for any dish if you asked them: a pinch of this
and a handful of that goes into most recipes so feel free to
do the same.

If you don't get time to try more than a few of the dishes
below, most of the ingredients are available here, so you can
make them at home.

SOUPS, SNACKS AND STARTERS

Soups

La zuppa del povero (poor man's soup)
Minestra alla menta (mint soup)
Minestrone (thick vegetable soup)
Risi e bisi (rice and peas)
Stracciatella (egg soup)
Zuppa di cozze (mussel soup)
Zuppa di fagioli alla Toscana (Tuscan bean soup)

Snacks and Starters

Caprese (*mozzarella* and tomato salad)
Crostini di fegatini (fried croutons with liver)
Frittata (Italian flat omelette)
Insalata di carciofi e formaggio (salad of raw artichokes and cheese)
Insalata di riso con cozze e funghi (rice salad with mussels and mushrooms)
Mozzarella in carrozza (fried *mozzarella* sandwiches)
Panne frattau (eggs and bread — Sardinian style)
Panzanella (Tuscan bread salad)
Prosciutto e melone (Parma ham with melon)
Uova alla provola (fried eggs with provola cheese)

RICE, PASTA, POLENTA AND GNOCCHI

Gnocchi alla Romana (semolina *gnocchi* with cheese)
Penne all'arrabbiata (angry or spicy *penne*)
Penne aromatiche (aromatic *penne*) (any sort of ready made tubular pasta can be substituted for the *penne*)
Polenta (maize pudding)
Riso col pomodoro e basilico (rice with tomato and basil)
Risotto alla Milanese (rice with saffron and white wine)
Risotto con asparagi (rice with fresh asparagus)
Spaghetti alla carbonara (spaghetti with eggs and bacon)
Spaghetti alla sporcaciona (dirty girl's spaghetti)
Spaghetti all'olio e aglio (spaghetti with oil and garlic)

VEGETABLE DISHES

Asparagi alla parmigiana (baked asparagus with Parmesan)
Carciofi stufati (stewed artichokes)
Finocchi saporiti al prosciutto (fennel cooked with ham)
Imbrogliata di carciofi (artichokes with eggs and cheese)
Lenticchie con le salsicce (lentils with sausages)
Melanzane alla parmigiana (baked aubergine/eggplant with *mozzarella*)
Patate alla diavola (spicy potatoes)
Patate alla Veneziana (potatoes fried in rosemary)
Peperonata (ratatouille of peppers)
Pomodori ripieni di riso (tomatoes stuffed with rice)
Zucchini al forno (courgettes/*zucchini*, baked with *mozzarella*)

SAUCES (FOR MEAT, FISH OR PASTA)

Pesto (basil sauce with garlic, cheese and pine nuts)
Pizzaiola (tomato and garlic sauce)
Ragu (Bolognese meat sauce)
Salsa verde (uncooked parsley sauce with capers)
Sugo di pomodoro alla Napoletana (tomato sauce from
   Naples)

MAIN COURSES

Fish

Calamari fritto (fried squid)
Coda di rospo (tail of monkfish or angler fish)
Pesce spada al salmoriglio (swordfish with oil and lemon)
Pesce spada in umido al vino (swordfish cooked in vegetables
   and wine)
Sarde alla Napoletana (baked sardines)
Scampi in umido (stewed prawns)
Spigola con timo, pomodoro e olive (sea bass with thyme,
   tomatoes and olives)
Triglie in cartoccio (mullet baked in tin foil)

Meat

Cervello al burro nero (brains with capers)
Fegato alla Veneziana (sliced liver with onions)
Fettine di manzo alla Sorrentina (beef escalopes with
   tomatoes and olives)
Osso buco alla Milanese (shin of veal)
Pollo alla Marengo (chicken in brandy and tomatoes)
Pollo tonnato (cold chicken with a tuna fish sauce)
Polpette al limone (lemon flavoured meatballs)
Polpettone alla casalinga (meat loaf)
Saltimbocca alla Romana (veal parcels with ham and sage)
Scaloppine ammantate (veal escalopes with *mozzarella*)
Trippa alla Livornese (tripe in oil and vinegar)

DESSERTS

Coppe di melone e anguria (melon and watermelon salad)
Crema di ricotta (cream of *ricotta* cheese)
Fichi al forno (baked figs)
Granita di caffè con panna (crushed coffee ice with cream)
Le bisse (snake-shaped biscuits)
Pere ripiene (pears stuffed with *Gorgonzola*)
Pesche al vino rosso (peaches in red wine)
Torta di marroni (chestnut cake)

SOUPS, SNACKS AND STARTERS

Soups

La zuppa del povero
(poor man's soup)

This is a very old recipe which probably originates in Tuscany and was eaten by the poor.

600g (1lb) greens
1½ litres (2½ pints) water or
  chicken stock
6 tablespoons olive oil

6 slices stale bread
6 tablespoons grated
  Parmesan cheese
Salt and pepper to taste

Heat the oven and wash the greens thoroughly. If the stems are tough cut off the hardest part and chop the rest into 1-inch pieces. Boil the water or chicken stock and add the greens. Cook, covered over for at least 1 hour then add the oil, salt and pepper. Place the slices of bread in the oven until golden and then put one slice in the bottom of each soup dish. Add four tablespoons of Parmesan cheese to the soup and let it cook for a further 10 minutes. Ladle the soup over the bread and sprinkle over the rest of the cheese. Serve piping hot.

Minestra alla menta
(mint soup)

This is a light soup and the mint gives it a fresh flavour. It should be served very hot and if you want to dress it up a bit, add some croutons or small pieces of fried bread.

1 small marrow (or pumpkin)
2 medium potatoes
2 carrots
3 celery sticks
1 small onion
1 leek

100g (3½oz) butter
¼litre (½ pint) cream
Grated nutmeg
4 sprigs fresh mint
Salt and pepper to taste

Clean, peel and chop the vegetables. Chop the mint into tiny pieces leaving a few whole leaves aside. Put all the vegetables and the chopped mint into a large saucepan with about 1 litre (about 2 pints) of water. Pour in the cream and some salt and pepper, cook for 15 minutes and then add a pinch of grated nutmeg. Stir and simmer for another 10 minutes and, just before serving, drop in the butter and the whole mint leaves. Bring it to the table piping hot.

Minestrone
(thick vegetable soup)

Every region in Italy makes its own version of *minestrone* — most include a little bacon and oil and, above all, as many fresh vegetables as possible. *Minestrone* is a filling and nutritious dish and as it is so thick, it really can be a meal in itself! This version is from Milan.

*60g (2oz) bacon (*pancetta *)*
1 clove garlic
1 large onion
2 celery sticks
2 carrots
*2 courgettes/*zucchini
½ cabbage
100g (3½oz) shelled peas
  (or frozen if unavailable)
2 medium potatoes
200g (7oz) ripe plum
  tomatoes (or a tin of
  peeled tomatoes)

200g (7oz) borlotti beans
  (fresh if possible,
  otherwise soak dried ones
  in cold water overnight)
100g (3½oz) rice
3 tablespoons freshly
  chopped parsley
30g (1oz) freshly grated
  Parmesan cheese
2 tablespoons olive oil
Salt and pepper to taste

Choose a large saucepan and put in the chopped onion, garlic and bacon with the oil. Fry until the onion is transparent but not brown. On a wooden board chop the vegetables including the parsley (but not the peas and beans!). Add the chopped carrots and celery to the saucepan and after about 2 or 3 minutes add the chopped potatoes and beans. Fry these together and after another 2 or 3 minutes put in all the other vegetables. Cover with cold water, add salt and paper, cover and cook on a low heat for about 2½ hours. Add the rice after about 2¼ hours as it only takes 18 minutes to cook. Remove from the heat and serve with grated Parmesan cheese.

Risi e bisi
(rice and peas)

This dish is a great favourite in Venice and used to be eaten in late spring during festivals, when Venice was a republic. It is a very thick soup which can almost be eaten with a fork. Fresh peas are by far the best, but frozen *petits pois* will do.

360g (12oz) rice
250g (8oz) shelled peas or 250g (8oz) frozen or tinned petits pois
1 medium onion
2 celery sticks
½ garlic clove
60g (2oz) butter

1 tablespoon vegetable oil
1½ litres (2½ pints) chicken stock
60g (2oz) grated Parmesan cheese
3 tablespoons chopped fresh parsley
Salt and pepper to taste

Pour the oil and half the butter into a saucepan and heat. Add the finely chopped onion, celery sticks and garlic clove and fry gently for 3 minutes or until the onion is transparent. Add the shelled peas and cook for about 10 minutes on a very low heat. If you use frozen peas, thaw them and fry them for only 3 minutes. Heat the chicken stock. Add the rice to the pan with the peas and stir, then, with a ladle, pour in the chicken stock and cover. Allow to cook for 18 minutes or until the rice is tender. Remove from the heat and add the last piece of butter, the chopped parsley, the salt and pepper and serve, piping hot, with grated Parmesan cheese sprinkled over it.

Stracciatella
(egg soup)

This light soup is made all over central Italy and is ideal for children, or for anyone feeling a little off colour.

60g (2oz) freshly grated breadcrumbs
60g (2oz), approximately, freshly grated Parmesan cheese
3 eggs

1½ litres (2½ pints) broth (home-made meat stock or a good broth cube)
2 tablespoons chopped parsley

Mix the eggs, the grated cheese and breadcrumbs in a bowl. Heat the broth in a saucepan and, when it simmers, pour a ladleful into the bowl and mix together to form a thick paste. Put the mixture into the saucepan and let it boil for one minute. The eggs will float to the surface, forming a feathery layer. Turn the heat right down and gently beat the soup with a fork for 2 minutes. Add the finely chopped parsley and serve immediately.

Zuppa di cozze
(mussel soup)

3 litres (5 pints) of mussels
1 kg (2¼lb) tomatoes
3 cloves of garlic
Celery
2 onions sliced
Fresh marjoram, thyme or
    basil

Ground black pepper
Glass of white wine
Parsley
Lemon juice

Take a deep pan and cover the bottom with olive oil, put in the sliced onions and when they begin to brown the herbs, sliced garlic and a spoonful of chopped celery. Cook for a few minutes and then add the skinned and sliced tomatoes. Stew for three or four minutes and add the glass of white wine, cook for another few minutes and then cover and simmer until tomatoes are reduced. Add a cup of boiling water and leave to simmer for a few more minutes. Let it stand until you are ready to serve.

Clean the mussels and remove the hair. Put them into the heated soup and cook fast until all are opened (10 minutes or so). Sprinkle parsley and lemon juice over the mussels before serving. Mop up with chunks of toasted bread.

Zuppa di fagioli alla Toscana
(Tuscan bean soup)

A highly nutritious and relatively easy soup eaten in Tuscany.

¼kg (½lb) white beans
    (cannellini)
Parsley

Garlic
Olive oil
Pepper and salt

Soak the beans in water overnight (but not more than about 12 hours or they will start to ferment and sprout!). Throw away the water. Add about 1½ litres (2½ pints) of cold water and simmer, covered, until they are tender. If they are the new season's beans they will take about 1½ hours, otherwise they may take as long as 3. When they are soft put half of them through a sieve (use the back of a wooden spoon) and return the purée to the saucepan. Chop up a few cloves of garlic and a few sprigs of parsley (go easy on the garlic if you're feeding children) and sautée gently in a little olive oil. Stir it into the soup, add salt and pepper and, just before serving, a little more olive oil.

SNACKS AND STARTERS

Caprese
(*mozzarella* and tomato salad)

4 *small* mozzarella *cheeses*	*Salt and pepper*
8 tomatoes	*Basil*
Fresh basil	*Oregano*
Olive oil	

Simple, and delicious — the best cheese to use is *bufalina* — *mozzarella* made with buffalo milk. Slice the *mozzarella* thinly and arrange on individual plates with thin slices of tomato. Pour a little olive oil over the top, season and sprinkle a little oregano and a few crushed basil leaves in the centre. It may not sound like much, but wait until you taste it.

Crostini di fegatini
(fried croutons with liver)

A quick and easy snack usually served before a meal in Tuscany and Umbria.

Stale bread	*Lemon juice*
360g (12oz) chicken livers	*Flour*
Smoked ham (slice)	*Stock*
Butter	

Chop up the livers (clean them carefully and remove any green bits), cover with flour. Cut up the ham and brown in butter, then put in the liver and cook gently. Add a few tea-spoonfuls of stock, season and add a drop of lemon juice. Cook for about ten minutes. Cut the crusts off the bread and cut into bite-sized squares. Fry in butter until crisp on the outside and soft in the middle. When done put on a dish and pour the livers over them.

If you don't want to use chicken livers you can invent your own topping; *mozzarella* and a jar of *pomodori sotto olio* — sun dried tomatoes is an alternative. Cut the bread into wedges, spread on the tomato until it soaks in, cover with slices of cheese and bake in a hot oven until it has melted.

Frittata
(Italian flat omelette)

Frittatas, unlike omelettes, can be cut into slices and served cold. A *frittata* enthusiast has a special frying pan exclusively for making them. It is never washed, just wiped clean. This version, with onions, is from the Veneto.

3 large onions	*40g (1½oz) butter*
8 eggs	*Salt and pepper to taste*
2 tablespoons vegetable oil	

Cut the onions into thin rings and fry until golden brown on a low heat in the oil and the butter. Add the salt, leave for 30 seconds and then pour in the beaten eggs. Turn the heat down and cook for about 8 minutes until the mixture is firm, but not hard. Turn the *frittata* over by putting a large plate over the pan and turning it upside down, then put it back for another minute. Serve hot or cold. Other variations use herbs, cheese or leftover *peperonata*.

Insalata di carciofi e formaggio (salad of raw artichokes and cheese)

It is very important to buy small and tender artichokes if you are going to eat them raw.

8 small, young artichokes	*2 lemons*
200g (7oz) emmental *cheese*	*Salt and pepper to taste*
2 tablespoons olive oil	
3 tablespoons freshly	
chopped parsley	

With a sharp knife cut off the stalks of the artichokes and remove the hard outer leaves. If necessary, cut off the prickly tips. Cut them lengthways into quarters and then cut again. As you prepare each artichoke put it into a bowl of cold water with a squeeze of lemon to stop it going black. Cut the *emmental* cheese into small cubes and put into a salad bowl. Take the artichokes out of the water, dry them and add to the cheese. Make the dressing with the lemons, olive oil and salt and pepper, pour it over the artichokes and cheese and sprinkle on the finely chopped parsley. Mix well and serve.

Insalata di riso con cozze e funghi (rice salad with mussels and mushrooms)

This unusual dish has a delicate flavour and is eaten in the summer, anywhere along the coast.

250g (8oz) arborio *rice*
800g (1 lb 12oz) mussels
250g (8oz) mushrooms
  (ovoli)
2 hard-boiled eggs (only the
  yolks)
4 tablespoons olive oil

3 drops Worcester sauce
  (optional)
¹/₂ lemon
2 tablespoons freshly
  chopped parsley
Salt and pepper to taste

Open the mussels by boiling them in water on maximum heat. Do not force open any mussels that are closed. Take out the mussels and put them aside. Carefully wash the mushrooms and then slice them very thinly. Boil the rice in salted water for 18 minutes and drain it, washing it with cold water under the tap so as to stop any further cooking. Drain the rice thoroughly and put it into a large bowl. Take two hard-boiled eggs and remove the yolk, mashing it with a fork in a small bowl. Add the olive oil, Worcester sauce and the juice from half a lemon and mix well. Put the mussels into the bowl with the rice, add salt and pepper and pour on the mixture with the egg yolks and add the mushrooms and parsley. Stir gently and put it into the fridge for an hour before serving.

Mozzarella in carrozza
(fried *mozzarella* sandwiches)

This is a very popular snack and literally means *mozzarella* in a carriage. It is quick and easy to make and is a great favourite with children.

200g (7oz) mozzarella
8 large slices of white bread
2 eggs
75g (2¹/₂oz) flour

2 tablespoons vegetable oil
225ml (8fl oz) milk
Salt and pepper to taste

Cut the bread into eight slices and remove the crust. Cut the *mozzarella* into eight slices and make four sandwiches with the bread and the cheese. In one bowl put the flour and in another break the eggs and add the milk with salt and pepper and mix thoroughly. In the meantime heat the oil in a large frying pan. Take one sandwich at a time and put it into the egg and milk mixture, so the mixture covers both sides. Then remove the sandwich quickly and put it in the bowl with the flour, turn it, so that the flour sticks. Quickly put the sandwich into the frying pan when the oil is very hot. You can probably fit two or three sandwiches into the pan at once. Fry until each sandwich is a golden brown colour all over, then place them on a piece of kitchen paper to remove any excess oil and serve.

Panne frattau
(eggs and bread − Sardinian style)

This dish, a favourite with Sardinian shepherds, is made with the flat unleavened *carta da musica* − one sheet should be enough per person but double up on eggs for heartier appetites. The bread originated in Sardinia but you can now get it all over Italy.

4 sheets of carta da musica	*Grated* pecorino *cheese*
4 soft-boiled eggs (peeled)	*Boiling water*
Fresh tomato sauce	

Take a large plate and put the sheets of *carta da musica* on it. Ladle over a few spoons of boiling water to soften the bread. Let it stand for a while. Lift the sheets off carefully to drain and put one on each plate (previously warmed). Squash the hot soft boiled egg onto the bread, add a spoonful or two of hot tomato sauce and some grated *pecorino*. Eat it with a knife and fork. You either like it or you don't!

Panzanella
(Tuscan bread salad)

Italians love bread. This particular recipe is a summer dish and is a meal in itself. *Panzanella* is an ancient dish eaten by peasants and is well suited to the bread of Tuscany which has no salt. The bread needs to be about 2 days old!

1 small loaf Tuscan bread	*6 black olives*
75 ml (3 fl oz) olive oil	*1 tablespoon capers*
2 tablespoons wine vinegar	*8 fresh basil leaves*
500 g (1 lb) ripe tomatoes	*2 tablespoons freshly*
1 small red onion	*chopped parsley*
1 garlic clove	*Salt and pepper to taste*

Break the bread into small chunks and put it into a deep bowl and cover with water. Let it soak for about 15 minutes. In the meantime remove the skin from the ripe tomatoes by putting them in boiling water for 2 minutes, then chop the tomatoes into small pieces and put them into another deep bowl (a salad bowl is ideal). With your hands, squeeze out the water from the bread and put it into the bowl with the tomatoes. Add the finely chopped onion, garlic, olive oil, vinegar and capers. Mix thoroughly. Tear the fresh basil leaves with your fingers and add them to the bread with the olives and parsley and sprinkle on some salt and pepper. Mix well and put it in the fridge for at least an hour before serving.

Prosciutto e melone
(Parma ham with melon)

This hardly needs a recipe but it's a reminder that this is not only one of the easiest *antipasti* to prepare but it is also one of the best. Arrange three or four fairly thin wedges of melon (cut off the skin) on a plate and drape thin slices of Parma ham over them. Italians sometimes eat their ham with butter. You need nothing else.

Uova alla provola
(fried eggs with *provola* cheese)

8 eggs	*Salt*
250g (8oz) provola *cheese*	*Butter*
Ground pepper	*Parmesan cheese*

Grease a large pan with butter. Put the sliced *provola* cheese on the bottom and break in the eggs. Sprinkle with salt, pepper, a little Parmesan and a few pieces of butter. Put in a hot oven until the cheese is gooey and the eggs cooked as much as you want them to be. Serve immediately. If you can't find *provola* or *provolone* use *fontina* or *scamorze*.

RICE, PASTA, POLENTA AND GNOCCHI

Gnocchi alla Romana
(semolina *gnocchi* with cheese)

Gnocchi make a delicious first course. There are many different types. The most famous *gnocchi* are from the area around Verona. In Naples they are called *strangolapreti*, which literally translated means priest stranglers! *Gnocchi* are usually made with potatoes and flour, some regions also add eggs. *Gnocchi alla Romana* are made with semolina and can be eaten with tomato, mushroom, or cheese and butter sauce.

250g (8oz) semolina
1 litre (1½ pints) milk
2 egg yolks
60g (2oz) butter

100g (3½oz) freshly grated
* Parmesan cheese*
60g (2oz) breadcrumbs
Salt to taste

Pour the milk and ½ litre (¾ pint) water into a large saucepan and add a pinch of salt. When the milk starts to boil, let the semolina trickle through your fingers into the milk and stir. Bring to the boil for 10 or 12 minutes and then remove from the heat. When the semolina has cooled down, add the egg yolks and half the grated cheese and stir. Pour the semolina onto a very large plate and spread it evenly with the blade of a knife, so it's about half an inch thick. Cut the semolina (which should be like a thick paste) into circles by using the hollow end of a small glass or cup. Take a large ovenproof dish and grease it thoroughly with half the butter. In a small bowl mix the breadcrumbs with the grated cheese. Put the semolina circles into the ovenproof dish, one layer at a time. Between each layer pour some of the grated cheese and breadcrumbs with one or two tiny chips of butter. Once all the semolina circles have been arranged in the dish, put it in a preheated oven for 15 minutes until a golden crust has formed. If the *gnocchi* are still bubbling they might be a little too soft, so let them cool down for 5 minutes and then serve.

Penne all'arrabbiata
(angry or spicy *penne*)

Penne are pasta tubes cut diagonally. This sauce is *arrabbiata* which means angry. The angrier the *penne* are, the more spicy they are — it is up to you! Without the added chilli or *peperoncini* the sauce is a plain tomato sauce which is made without any butter or oil. This is a useful tomato sauce as it can be used on any pasta dish or poured over a steak, making it *alla pizzaiola*!

400g (14oz) penne
500g (1lb) plum tomatoes or
*   a can of peeled tomatoes*
1 celery stick
1 small onion
1 garlic clove

2½cm (1 inch) chilli
*   (peperoncino)*
1 tablespoon freshly
*   chopped parsley*
Salt and pepper to taste

While the *penne* are cooking chop the celery, the onion and the garlic clove. Put them into a medium saucepan with the can of peeled tomatoes (you can cut the tomatoes with a fork), or if you are using fresh tomatoes, put them in a bowl of boiling water for 3 or 4 minutes so the skin lifts off easily and then chop them up. Cut the *peperoncino* and remove the seeds. Chop it into small pieces and add it to the sauce with salt and pepper to taste. Cook, uncovered, over a medium heat for about 30 minutes so the sauce thickens. Drain the *penne*, put them into a large bowl and pour on the sauce. Sprinkle with fresh parsley, mix and serve.

Penne aromatiche
(aromatic *penne*)

This is an ideal and unusual way to prepare *penne* (or other tubular pasta) if you are staying on the coast or in the countryside. You will be able to pick many of your own herbs growing wild, those you are not sure of or can't find, buy locally.

400g (14oz) penne
3 tablespoons plain tomato
*   sauce*
3 tablespoons olive oil
1 garlic clove

2 fresh mint leaves
8 fresh basil leaves
4 sprigs fresh parsley
6 large black olives
Salt and pepper to taste

In a small saucepan fry the chopped garlic clove in olive oil, until it becomes golden brown — don't let it burn or it will have a bitter taste. Add the tomato sauce and 6 tablespoons of cold water and mix with salt and pepper, then let it cook on a low heat for 15 minutes. In the meantime chop the various herbs and the black olives (cut round the stones) and when the tomato sauce is ready, add the herbs and olives. Mix and let it cook for another 5 minutes. Drain the pasta thoroughly and put it into a large bowl. Pour over the sauce, mix and serve immediately (it is usually served without grated cheese).

Polenta
(maize pudding)

Polenta is a nourishing rich yellow dish from Piedmont and the Veneto. It used to be the staple diet of farmers in the Alps and is usually served with stews or game or eaten with milk as though it were bread. *Polenta* is easy to make but takes time and energy, so it is usually made in bulk — the leftovers can be fried with melted cheese and eaten the next day. The traditional *accoutrements* for making *polenta* are a large copper cauldron, a log fire to cook it over, a long wooden spoon and a wooden board on which to serve it. *Polenta* goes very well with game stews, *pollo alla cacciatora* and all fowl.

360g (12oz) coarse grained   1¹/₃ litres (2¹/₂ pints) water
*   cornmeal or polenta flour   2 teaspoons salt*

Take a large, heavy saucepan and fill with water, adding the salt. Just before the water boils sprinkle in the flour, letting it run through your fingers. Stir vigorously with a long wooden spoon, the longer the handle the better, as the mixture will bubble and splash you. It is very important to keep stirring so lumps don't form. Simmer and stir for about 20 minutes until the *polenta* comes easily away from the sides of the saucepan. Turn onto a wooden board and spread it into a dome-shaped heap. Serve hot.

Riso col pomodoro e basilico
(rice with tomato and basil)

This is a light and tasty first course ideal for children. Use fresh basil. The tomato sauce is also very plain and can be adapted to make many kinds of sauces.

360g (12oz) rice (arborio)   60g (2oz) butter
500g (1lb) plum tomatoes or   1 sprig fresh basil
*   a can of peeled tomatoes   Salt and pepper to taste*
2 tablespoons olive oil

While the rice is boiling, put the tomatoes in a bowl of boiling water for 2 minutes so the skin can be removed more easily.

Chop the tomatoes into small cubes and put them into a medium saucepan, together with their juice and the olive oil. Simmer for about 10 minutes. Drain and wash the rice by pouring cold water over it briefly, then put the rice into individual bowls. Add a little salt and pepper to the tomato sauce and pour it over the rice. Break the fresh basil leaves with your fingers and sprinkle over the rice, then add a blob of butter and serve.

Risotto alla Milanese
(rice with saffron and white wine)

This risotto is a beautiful golden colour because of the saffron. A good quality beef broth cube can be just as good as a home-made meat stock, and is much quicker. The dry white wine gives a delicious subtle flavour but is not essential. If, however, you do use wine, serve the same wine with the meal.

1½ litres (2½ pints) broth
1 small onion
360g (12oz) rice (preferably
 arborio)
Saffron (buy a small sachet
 at your local supermarket)

60g (2oz) freshly grated
 Parmesan cheese
75g (2½oz) butter
75ml (3floz) dry white wine
Salt and pepper to taste

Put a couple of broth cubes in a saucepan with water and bring to the boil. Take a large frying pan and put in the finely chopped onion with half the butter and fry until the onion is transparent. Pour in the rice and mix so that each grain is well covered in the butter. Once the rice is shiny add a ladleful of the broth and the rest of the butter. Pour in the wine and mix, adding the broth little by little as it becomes absorbed, never let the rice dry out and stir at frequent intervals. The risotto will take about 18 minutes. After 15 minutes add a generous pinch of saffron, the salt and pepper and mix. When the rice is cooked, remove from the heat and add the cheese. Stir well and serve piping hot.

Risotto con asparagi
(rice with fresh asparagus)

This risotto dish is a speciality of Venice where it is called *risotto coi sparasi*. To clean the asparagus, scrape the lower parts with a sharp knife to remove woody bits and earth. Wash thoroughly or soak to remove sand from tips. If you decide to add the white wine (optional) drink the same variety with the meal.

700g (1½lb) asparagus
360g (12oz) rice (arborio)
1 medium onion
2 tablespoons vegetable oil
75g (2½oz) butter
1½ litres (2½ pints) broth
   (chicken stock or a cube)

60g (2oz) freshly grated
   Parmesan
75ml (3floz) dry white wine
Salt and pepper

Put the broth or cube in a saucepan and bring to the boil. Cut the woody ends off the asparagus (can be used for soup) and chop the rest into 1-inch pieces. Heat the butter and oil in a large frying pan and add the finely chopped onion. When it becomes transparent add the pieces of asparagus, but keep back the tips. Mix well. Add the rice and stir until each grain is coated in butter, add the wine, stir until the liquid evaporates. Then add the broth a ladle at a time, never allowing the rice to become dry. After about 10 minutes add the asparagus tips and continue to stir, still adding broth. The risotto will take about 18 minutes to cook. A few minutes before serving, season, add the cheese and mix thoroughly.

Spaghetti alla carbonara
(spaghetti with eggs and bacon)

This easy dish is named after the charcoal burners (*carbonari*) who used to work in the forests of the Apennine mountains that run down the centre of Italy. For extra flavour use two types of freshly grated cheese such as Parmesan and *caciotta* or *pecorino*.

400g (14oz) spaghetti
100g (3½oz) bacon
   (pancetta)
2 egg yolks
60g (2oz) freshly grated
   Parmesan and caciotta or
   pecorino cheese

(30g about 1oz each)
1 tablespoon vegetable oil
Salt and black pepper to
   taste

While the spaghetti is cooking take a large frying pan and chop the bacon into small cubes and fry over a low heat until it is pale brown, not crisp. Beat the egg yolks and the two types of grated cheese in a small bowl and add some salt and plenty of black pepper. Drain the pasta well and pour it into the frying pan and mix with the bacon and oil. Finally add the egg and cheese mixture and stir well. Serve immediately.

Spaghetti alla sporcaciona
(dirty girl's spaghetti)

Italian recipes often have colourful names and this is one of them! *Sporcaciona* literally means dirty girl or slut, because the cook can't be bothered with saucepans and is too lazy to spend a long time preparing a sauce. It is a delicious sauce, very easy to make and above all there are no saucepans to wash up afterwards.

400g (14oz) spaghetti
8 ripe plum tomatoes (or a
  tin of peeled tomatoes)
75g (2½oz) mozzarella
1 tablespoon capers

8 large black olives
1 garlic clove
1 sprig fresh basil
4 tablespoons olive oil
Salt and pepper to taste

While the pasta is cooking cut the *mozzarella* into small cubes and put it into a large bowl. If you're using fresh tomatoes, put them in boiling water for 2 or 3 minutes so the skins lift off easily. Chop the tomatoes and garlic into small pieces and add to the cheese. Add the capers, whole olives, whole basil leaves, olive oil, salt and pepper and mix well. When the pasta is cooked drain it thoroughly and pour it into the bowl with the sauce. Stir until the *mozzarella* begins to melt and become stringy. Serve immediately.

Spaghetti all'olio e aglio
(spaghetti with oil and garlic)

This simple spaghetti dish is very popular around Rome and Naples and is strictly for garlic lovers!

400g (14oz) spaghetti
2 garlic cloves (minimum)
6 tablespoons olive oil

Salt and pepper to taste
1 tablespoon chopped
  parsley (optional)

While the spaghetti is cooking, chop the garlic cloves as small as possible and put them in a large frying pan with the olive oil and fry over a low heat. Remember not to let the garlic burn or it will be very bitter, it should be slightly brown. Add two tablespoons cold water and stir. When the spaghetti is ready, drain it well and add it to the garlic and oil in the frying pan. Mix well and leave for 1 or 2 minutes over a low heat and then serve with a little salt and pepper. If you like you can add a tablespoon of chopped parsley.

VEGETABLE DISHES

Asparagi alla parmigiana
(baked asparagus with Parmesan)

A good dish if you've missed the first of the season's tender asparagus or if you're using the fat asparagus from Tuscany which hasn't as much flavour as the wild asparagus from around Rome. A speciality of Parma *unlike* many other dishes with the same name.

1 kg (2¹/₄lb) asparagus	*75 g (2¹/₂oz) butter*
60 g (2 oz) freshly grated Parmesan	*Salt*

Depending on how tender the asparagus is you will have to cut away some of the stem and some of the tough fibrous stalk. Also trim any small leaves. Soak in cold water for about 10 minutes then rinse twice in fresh water.

Tie the asparagus up in a bundle in two places. If your villa doesn't run to a special asparagus pan or even a fish kettle (which would do) fill a deep oval pan with about 4 litres (7 pints) of water, bring it to the boil and place the asparagus bundle down flat inside it, boiling uncovered for about 15 minutes or until it is done enough to be pierced with a fork.

Lift the bundle out and transfer to a dish, untie the string and tip the dish so the juice runs to one end, throw it away.

If you have one, choose a rectangular dish the size of the asparagus and smear it with butter. Put a layer of asparagus along the bottom (all facing the same way). Sprinkle with salt, a dot of butter and grated Parmesan and then start another row, slightly overlapping, with the tips of the new row over the butts of the old one. Continue until used up but don't cover the tips.

Bake on the top shelf of a hot oven for about 15 minutes until golden.

Carciofi stufati
(stewed artichokes)

Not a dish you see much outside Italy, but it goes very well with meat or poultry. Choose small young artichokes.

8 small artichokes	*2 anchovy fillets*
1 clove of garlic	*Lemon juice*
6 tablespoons vegetable oil	*Salt and pepper to taste*
2 tablespoons wine vinegar	

Trim and quarter the artichokes, removing the hairy choke if there is any. Cut the sharp points off the leaves and all but 1 inch of the stem. Put the quarters in a bowl of water with lemon juice to prevent them from discolouring. Put the quarters in a pan with the oil, vinegar, chopped garlic, salt, pepper and six tablespoons of cold water. Cover and cook over a low heat for about 50 minutes. Remove the artichokes and keep warm. Put the anchovy fillets into the juice left in the pan, and mash with a wooden spoon. If it seems a little dry, add two tablespoons of cold water. Stir well, put the artichokes back in, mix and serve.

Finocchi saporiti al prosciutto
(fennel cooked with ham)

This unusual way of cooking fennel makes a delicious first course.

3/4 medium fennel	*2 tablespoons vegetable oil*
150g (5oz) ham	*60g (2oz) butter*
1 small onion	*60ml (2fl oz) stock (either*
60g (2oz) freshly grated	*meat or chicken)*
emmental cheese	*Salt and pepper to taste*
60g (2oz) freshly grated	
Parmesan cheese	

Cut away the green stalks and the tough outer leaves or layers. Cut the fennel lengthways into segments and wash carefully so they don't come apart. Take a wide saucepan and put in the oil, butter and finely chopped onion. Let this fry on a very low heat until the onion has become transparent and very limp — it must not be crisp. Chop the ham into small pieces and add them to the onion, stir and then add the fennel segments. Leave to fry gently for 2 minutes so the fennel can absorb the flavour of the ham, then pour in the stock. Add a pinch of salt and a little pepper and cook, covered, until the stock has been absorbed. Just before serving add the grated *emmental* and Parmesan cheese. Cover and let the cheese melt over the fennel for about 3 minutes, then serve piping hot and bubbling.

Imbrogliata di carciofi
(artichokes with eggs and cheese)

A speciality of Genoa that uses the tender artichokes of the Ligurian Riviera, served piping hot as a first course or to accompany a rather uneventful main dish.

4 artichokes	1/2 lemon
4 eggs	Salt to taste
60g (2oz) butter	
60g (2oz) freshly grated Parmesan	

Trim the artichokes including the outer leaves and cut length-ways into quarters, cutting away the hairy choke if there is any. Put them into a bowl of water with a little lemon juice to stop discolouring. Then slice as thinly as possible. Melt the butter in a frying pan and cook (add salt) over a moderate heat. Stir gently and add a teaspoonful of water. Fry for about 4 minutes.

In the meantime beat the eggs with the grated cheese and a pinch of salt, then slowly pour the mixture into the pan, turn up the heat and stir. After 3 minutes remove and serve.

Lenticchie con le salsiccie
(lentils with sausages)

This nutritious dish is very filling and a meal in itself!

250g (8oz) lentils	1 garlic clove
8 sausages	2 bay leaves
1 carrot	1/2 litre (1/4 pint) water
1 medium onion	Salt and pepper to taste

Soak the lentils in cold water for 12 hours and then drain. Pierce the sausages with a fork so they don't burst while cooking and soak for 2 minutes in a bowl of boiling water to remove any excess grease. Take a large saucepan and put in the lentils. Chop the carrot, the onion and the garlic and add to the lentils. Pour in about half a litre of water and the bay leaves. Add salt and pepper and cook, covered, for 10 minutes over a low heat and then add the sausages. Cook over a low heat for a further 30 minutes and serve piping hot.

Melanzane alla parmigiana
(baked aubergine/eggplant with mozzarella)

This is not the quickest of dishes but it is well worth taking a bit of time over. If you double up the quantities you can make two lots and then just put it in the oven or under the grill to heat up.

*1½kg (3lb) aubergines/
    eggplant*
2 small mozzarella *cheeses*
60g (2oz) Parmesan
*120ml (¼ pint) fresh
    tomato sauce*

6 tablespoons olive oil
Oregano
Flour
Salt and pepper

Choose smooth skinned shiny aubergines/eggplants. Wash and cut lengthways into thin slices. Salt and leave to drain for an hour or so in a colander. Dust with flour. Heat olive oil and fry each piece gently, setting aside on kitchen paper. Do not add more oil while the aubergines/eggplant are in the pan. Put a little oil in the bottom of a baking dish and put in a layer of aubergines/eggplants. Add thin slices of *mozzarella* and then the tomato and oregano. Build up the layers, and finish with tomato. Cover with freshly grated Parmesan, sprinkle with a little oil and bake in a moderate oven for about half an hour. Eat immediately. It isn't quite as good prepared in advance, but almost.

Patate alla diavola
(spicy potatoes)

This is an unusual way to serve potatoes and if you like spicy things just add more chillies. *Alla diavola* means 'as the devil eats' — in other words 'hot', so be warned!

1kg (2¼lb) potatoes
5 tablespoons olive oil
*2½cm (1 inch) fresh chilli
    (peperoncino)*

2 garlic cloves
Salt to taste

Boil the potatoes whole in their skins for about 15 minutes. Drain the water and peel — the skins will come away very easily. Slice the potatoes, but not too thinly. Heat the oil in a pan (the saucepan you used for boiling the potatoes will do) and add the chilli which you have seeded and chopped, together with the chopped garlic. Fry for 2 to 3 minutes until the garlic is a pale golden colour — don't let it burn or it will become bitter. Add the sliced potatoes and a pinch of salt. Turn the potatoes over till they become golden brown on both sides.

Patate alla Veneziana
(potatoes fried in rosemary)

This potato dish goes well with grilled fish, roast meats, chicken or veal. If you can, use fresh rosemary.

1 kg (2¼lb) potatoes
5 tablespoons olive oil
1 small onion

1 sprig of fresh rosemary or
  1 teaspoon dried
  rosemary
Salt and pepper to taste

Peel the potatoes and cut them into 1-inch cubes. Heat the olive oil in a frying pan and fry the potatoes over a low heat. Chop the onion into thin rings and add to the pan, turn up the heat and add the rosemary, salt and pepper. Fry for about 20 minutes, stirring occasionally until all sides are brown.

Peperonata
(ratatouille of peppers)

Peperonata is very like the French ratatouille but is made without onions. It can be eaten hot as a dish in itself, it goes very well with boiled, grilled or roast meats, with fish or as a sauce for spaghetti. Cold it can be eaten like a salad. If you are feeling artistic you can choose just two colours of peppers such as red and yellow.

500g (1lb) peppers
4 tablespoons olive oil
6 plum tomatoes (or a can
  of peeled tomatoes with
  the juice)

1 garlic clove
1 tablespoon freshly
  chopped parsley
Salt and pepper to taste

Remove the stems and seeds from the peppers and cut into long strips about half an inch wide. Heat the oil in a large frying pan and then add the peppers and garlic, stirring frequently for about 3 or 4 minutes. If you use fresh tomatoes place in boiling water to remove the skins, then chop them up adding them (with the juice) to the peppers. Season and stir. Cover and cook on a low heat for about 30 minutes or until the peppers are tender. Then add the parsley and serve.

Pomodori ripieni di riso
(tomatoes stuffed with rice)

Stuffed vegetables are very popular and this brightly coloured dish goes particularly well with grilled fish.

4 large tomatoes (or 8 smaller ones)	*1 tablespoon freshly chopped parsley*
200g (7oz) arborio *rice*	*60g (2oz) butter*
3 tablespoons olive oil	*salt and pepper to taste*
1 clove chopped garlic	

Wash the tomatoes and cut off the tops, setting them aside to use later as lids. Scoop out the pulp and seeds from the tomatoes with a teaspoon and put the pulp in a bowl. Sprinkle a little salt and pepper on to each tomato and put it upside down to drain. In the meantime cook the rice in salted boiling water for 10 minutes so it is only half cooked. Take an oven-proof dish large enough to accommodate all the tomatoes and grease it well with the butter. Mash the pulp with a fork and add the finely chopped garlic, parsley, olive oil and salt and pepper. Mix in the drained rice. With a teaspoon fill each tomato with the pulp and rice mixture and put the tomato top back on each, then place the tomatoes in the dish and bake them in the oven on a medium heat for about 30 minutes or until tender. Pierce the tomato with the point of a knife to see if it is done — the skin should be slightly wrinkled.

Zucchini al forno
(courgettes/*zucchini* baked with *mozzarella*)

A simpler version of *melanzane alla parmigiana*. Quick and easy — if you've got an oven.

500g (1lb) courgettes/ zucchini	*300g (10oz) tomatoes (plum variety are best)*
200g (7oz) mozzarella	*Parsley and Oregano*
2 eggs	*Olive oil*

Cut the courgettes/*zucchini* into slices lengthways. Butter a pan and put half on the bottom. Then half of the tomatoes, sliced up, a little parsley and some oregano. Cover with the remaining courgettes/*zucchini* and tomato. Add salt, several spoonfuls of olive oil and bake in a moderate oven for about 15 minutes or until the courgettes/*zucchini* are soft. When they are almost done, take out and cover with sliced *mozzarella* and the beaten egg. Replace for 5 minutes and serve hot.

SAUCES

Pesto
(basil sauce with garlic, cheese and pine nuts)

A speciality of Genoa, a powerful green sauce for pasta (long strands of spaghetti are best), soup or grilled fish. You really need a blender or a pestle and mortar to make it properly. (Well worth taking fresh basil and pine nuts home and making it there.)

$2^{1}/_{2}$ cups of fresh basil leaves
6 shelled walnuts (optional)
50g (1 tablespoonful) pine nuts
2 sliced cloves of garlic
10 tablespoonfuls of olive oil
1 tablespoon of butter

30g (1 oz) freshly grated Parmesan
30g (1 oz) freshly grated pecorino (or another ounce or two of Parmesan)
Salt and pepper

Exact quantities really depend on your taste. Go easy on the garlic to start with.

Blend or pound the basil, nuts, garlic and about four table-spoons of oil, slowly adding in the rest of the oil. Add the grated cheese and a tablespoonful of softened butter and keep pounding until it is the consistency of thick cream. Cover with foil and let it stand.

Pizzaiola
(tomato and garlic sauce)

This Neapolitan sauce is ideal for thin slices of beef or veal, particularly if they are a bit tough. It is also good on chops, meat balls or even fish.

700g (1$^{1}/_{2}$lb) ripe tomatoes
Oregano or basil
3 or 4 cloves of garlic

Olive oil
Salt and pepper
Few black olives (optional)

Peel (by immersing in boiling water for a few minutes) and slice the tomatoes, chop and add to the garlic and herbs sautéed in a little olive oil. Do not overcook. Spread the sauce over the escalopes. I always like to add a few sliced black olives too.

Ragu
(Bolognese meat sauce)

Ragu can be made in advance and kept in the fridge for about four days. The sauce can be used simply over spaghetti or to make *lasagne*.

180g (6oz) lean mince	*3 teaspoons of tomato purée*
90g (3oz) chicken livers	*Glass of red or white wine*
60g (2oz) pancetta —	*2 glasses of stock or water*
streaky bacon	*Butter*
A carrot	*Salt and pepper*
An onion	*Nutmeg*
Small stick of celery	*Freshly grated Parmesan*

Brown the cut up bacon in 15g (½oz) of butter in a small saucepan. Add the finely chopped vegetables and when brown the raw mince. Brown evenly and then add the chicken livers, cook for a few minutes and add the tomato purée and the white wine, season, add the nutmeg (just a scraping), the water or stock, cover and simmer for about 40 minutes. To serve mix it with the hot pasta and add a blob of butter. Let each person add their own Parmesan.

Salsa verde
(uncooked parsley sauce with capers)

This is a delicious sauce served traditionally with *bollito misto* (boiled meats), but is ideal for making any plain boiled or grilled fish more exciting. It even goes well with halved hard-boiled eggs. It is very simple to make and you don't have to cook it. As it is a thick, rather sharp sauce it can be toned down by adding a small boiled potato — this also gives it more body. You need plenty of Italian parsley. *Salsa verde* can be stored, covered over, in the fridge for about 2 weeks.

A bunch of parsley	*100ml (4floz) olive oil*
2 anchovy fillets	*½ teaspoon French mustard*
1 garlic clove	*1 small boiled potato*
1 tablespoon capers	*(optional)*
1 tablespoon lemon juice	

Chop the parsley and garlic on a wooden board. In a bowl mash the capers, anchovy fillets and small boiled potato (if you need one). Add the lemon juice and French mustard and mix well — do not use an electric blender or mixer as the sauce should be fairly coarse. Add the parsley and garlic to the bowl and slowly pour in the olive oil, stirring all the time. The anchovy fillets should provide all the salt you need.

Sugo di pomodoro alla Napoletana (tomato sauce from Naples)

The simplest of the tomato sauces, but it does use a fair bit of olive oil.

*500g (1lb) fresh or canned
    tomatoes*
*1 clove of garlic (crushed or
    chopped)*
*Fresh basil leaves (torn or
    chopped)*

5 tablespoons olive oil
Salt
Freshly ground black pepper

Put the tomatoes, olive oil, garlic, basil, salt and pepper in a small saucepan and simmer over a moderate heat for about 10 minutes or until the oil has separated from the tomatoes. If you are using fresh tomatoes add a couple of tablespoon-fuls of water. If you're not too keen on olive oil, omit it and add instead a chopped up onion, a small chopped up stick of celery and a bay leaf and simmer for about half an hour. Push the sauce through a sieve or mouli. You can keep it in the fridge for a few days.

MAIN COURSES

Fish

Calamari fritto
(fried squid)

1 kg (2¼lb) baby squid　　*Olive oil*
Flour　　　　　　　　　　*Lemon*
Salt, pepper

Buy small squid (for cleaning see main squid entry). Cut the sacs into rings and cut up the tentacles. Dip into seasoned flour. Heat oil until it begins to smoke. Fry the rings until they are crisp and golden and serve with wedges of lemon.

Coda di rospo
(tail of monkfish or angler fish)

A Venetian speciality although the fish is common all over the Adriatic. An ugly creature, that has a thick firm flesh that tastes a bit like lobster. The heads are usually removed and the tails sold separately.

　　Buy a largish tail and simply split it in half. Grill for about 20 minutes, turning over half way. Serve with a wedge of lemon or a *salmoriglio* sauce (see following swordfish recipe).

Pesce spada al salmoriglio
(swordfish with oil and lemon)

Swordfish steaks are thick and chunky and have little bone. Cooking them this way ensures they don't dry out. Don't be put off by the red colour, they turn white as soon as they start to cook. The sauce is a Sicilian one (swordfish swarm past the island in droves in early summer), and can be used for other thick fleshed fish, lobster tails, turbot, halibut and tuna. It is quick, easy and incredibly good!

900g (2lb) or four swordfish　*1 teaspoon oregano*
*　steaks sliced fairly thinly*　*4 tablespoons of olive oil*
2 tablespoons freshly　　　*Pepper*
*　squeezed lemon juice*

Make the sauce about an hour before the meal. Put the lemon juice and a pinch of salt into a bowl and beat with a fork, trickling in the olive oil until it all blends together. Add the pepper.

Heat the grill as hot as you can get it. Put the steaks under for a couple of minutes each side — they do not have to brown, simply be cooked through. Transfer to a warm dish and pour the sauce over, basting it onto individual plates as you serve. Cooking tip: the fish smell quite strong, so it's worth putting silver foil under them or the pan will keep the smell for ages.

Pesce spada in umido al vino
(swordfish cooked in vegetables and wine)

Swordfish is a very tasty fish and, as you buy it in large steaks, you throw away very little. It does not have a particularly fishy flavour and is equally good grilled or cooked with a tomato sauce.

4 swordfish steaks	360g (12oz) shelled peas
1 onion	(or a tin if unavailable)
1 garlic clove	Tin peeled tomatoes
2 tablespoons freshly	4 tablespoons vegetable oil
chopped parsley	60g (2oz) butter
100ml (4floz) red wine	Salt and pepper to taste

Gently fry the chopped onion, garlic and parsley in the butter and oil. In the meantime wash and dry the swordfish steaks and, when the onion has become slightly transparent, put in the fish. Cook for about 8 minutes (4 minutes on each side) until the fish is pale golden, add the salt and pepper and the red wine. Once the wine has evaporated add the peas (if they are fresh they must be very tender — if not use a tin of *petits pois*). Carefully mix the peas, onions and fish and let them cook together on a low heat for 2 or 3 minutes before adding the tin of tomatoes. Turn the swordfish over, mix in the tomatoes and cook, covered, on a low heat for about 30 minutes and then serve.

Sarde alla Napoletana
(baked sardines)

Fresh sardines taste nothing like the tinned variety. Buy smallish ones and ask the fishmonger to bone them for you — but try and keep them joined at the tail! This quick and easy dish brings out the flavour of the fresh sardines.

1 kg (2¹/₄lb) sardines　　*Clove of garlic*
Olive oil　　　　　　　　*Oregano*
Chopped parsley　　　　*2 or 3 tomatoes*

Slit the sardines in half, keeping them joined at the tail and remove the backbone, guts and head. Rinse and pat dry on kitchen paper.

Put some oil in the bottom of a flat (if possible oval) dish and place the open sardines in it. You may need two layers. Season and add the chopped garlic and parsley, a pinch of oregano and chunks of peeled tomato.

Pour over a little more olive oil and cook in a hot oven (430F, gas 7) for about 20 minutes.

Scampi in umido
(stewed prawns)

1 kg (2¹/₄lb) of prawns (as　　*Chopped parsley*
　　first course, double for　　*Chopped garlic*
　　main course)　　　　　　*A few capers*
Olive oil　　　　　　　　　*Lemon juice*

Buy fresh uncooked prawns and peel them. Sautée in the olive oil in a thick pan and after 10 minutes add the chopped garlic, a handful of parsley, a few capers and a squeeze of lemon juice. Serve as an *antipasto* in their own little dishes (if you've got them) and mop the juices up with bread, or with boiled rice as a main course.

Spigola con timo, pomodoro e olive
(sea bass with thyme, tomatoes and olives)

Sea bass has a thick white flesh; this baked dish takes little time to prepare.

700g (1¹/₂lb) sea bass,　　　*1¹/₂ tablespoons of olive oil*
　　filleted with skin removed　*9 pitted black olives*
700g (1¹/₂lb) fresh tomatoes　*Salt and pepper*

Skin and mash (or push through a sieve) the tomatoes and put them with the olive oil, thyme, olives and seasoning in a baking dish. Arrange the fillets close to one another and place in a very hot oven. Bake until the fish flakes easily with a fork — which will be sooner than you'd expect.

Triglie in cartoccio
(mullet baked in tin foil)

Mullet is a delicious reddish fish with a delicate flavour but as it is rather fragile, handle it carefully while cooking. True connoisseurs say that it doesn't have to be gutted as its liver is very good and it doesn't have a gall bladder.

Italians have been cooking in foil or greaseproof paper for years to keep in all the natural goodness — serve the fish at the table in the foil and let each person open his own 'parcel'.

4 large mullet   *60g (2oz) butter*
2 sprigs fresh rosemary *2 tablespoons vegetable oil*
½ lemon   *Salt and pepper to taste*

Wash and dry the fish. If they are rather big, make one or two small incisions with a sharp knife along the backs, this will ensure that they won't split while cooking. In the belly put half a sprig of fresh rosemary, a blob of butter and some salt and pepper. Wrap each fish loosely in tin foil putting a little oil in each parcel and a thin slice of lemon. Just roll and pinch the foil to close it. Place the parcels of fish in a large ovenproof dish or baking tray, remember you don't have to put any oil or butter in the dish as everything is inside the parcels. Put the fish in a preheated oven and cook on a medium to high heat for 20 minutes and serve.

Meat

Cervello al burro nero
(brain with capers)

Brain is a very delicate and light dish and goes well with
bland vegetables like mashed potatoes. If they seem too
bland, squeeze a little lemon over them or even some dry
white wine. The most important thing is that they should be
eaten fresh.

700g (1½lb) veal's brain
100g (3½oz) butter
1 tablespoon capers
75ml (3floz) white wine or
  wine vinegar

1 tablespoon parsley
Salt and pepper to taste

Soak the brains in a bowl of warm water for three quarters of
an hour and then clean off any blood vessels with your
fingers, it's not as bad as it sounds! Dry the brains in a piece
of kitchen paper and cut them into egg-sized pieces. Take a
frying pan and melt the butter until it becomes brown, then
add the pieces of brain and cook, turning them over regularly, for 10 minutes. Sprinkle on salt, pepper and parsley
and place on a serving dish. Add the capers and the white
wine or vinegar to the melted butter in which the brains have
been frying, and pour this over the brains and serve. If you
use white wine, drink the same wine with the meal.

Fegato alla Veneziana
(sliced liver with onions)

Although this dish is typical of the Veneto it is eaten all over
Italy. Use calf's liver as it is the most tender and if you decide
to cook it in wine, serve the same wine with the meal.

700g (1½lb) calf's liver
2 large onions
4 tablespoons vegetable oil
60g (2oz) butter
3 tablespoons freshly
  chopped parsley

100ml (4floz) dry white
  wine (optional)
Salt and pepper to taste

Melt the butter and oil in a frying pan. Chop the onions into
thin rings and fry them on a low heat until they are transparent, not brown. Slice the calf's liver into thin strips and

add them to the onions. If you are using white wine, pour it in. Mix with a wooden spoon and make sure that the liver cooks on both sides — it should be slightly pink inside, don't let it become hard and grey, cook it *slowly* for about 10 minutes. Just before serving, add the chopped parsley.

Fettine di manzo alla Sorrentina
(beef escalopes with tomatoes and olives)

You can use thin slices of beef or *scaloppine* of veal for this recipe, which looks quite dramatic with the red tomatoes and black olives. It doesn't take long to prepare either.

500g (1lb) of steak (fettine)
pounded flat
Small onion
2 cloves of garlic
Small tin of tomatoes with
juice

12 pitted black olives
Oregano
Pepper

Prepare the sauce first. Slice the onion and sautée gently in olive oil until soft. Add the diced garlic and the chopped tomatoes, the quartered olives and a pinch of oregano. Season, stir and simmer for about a quarter of an hour. Cover until you need it. (It will keep well in the fridge.)

Cut the meat into smallish squares and notch the edges so it doesn't curl up. Fry quickly, season, transfer the meat to the sauce which should be warming in another pan. Baste and transfer it all to a hot serving dish.

Osso buco alla Milanese
(*shin of veal*)

This delicious dish is a speciality of Lombardy and is served with *risotto alla Milanese*.

Shin of veal is used for this, so remember to scoop out the marrow with a teaspoon as it is very tasty and nutritious. You may need two *ossi buchi* each as they are not always meaty.

8 ossi buchi (veal shins) 1.6
kg (3½lb) approximately
1 small onion
60g (2oz) butter
2 tablespoons vegetable oil
3 tablespoons flour
300ml (½ pint) meat stock

150ml (¼ pint) dry white
wine
1 lemon rind
1 tablespoon freshly
chopped parsley
1 garlic clove
Salt and pepper to taste

Check that each *osso buco* is fairly compact, if not secure a piece of string around the diameter of each piece.

Put the flour on a plate and coat the meat on both sides. Take a frying pan large enough to hold all the meat tightly packed, but not overlapping. Chop the onion into thin rings and fry it in the pan with the butter and oil. When the onion is slightly transparent put in the *ossi buchi* and brown on both sides. Season with salt and pepper and pour in the wine, turn the heat up for 5 minutes, turning the meat over regularly. Add the stock and cover over for 2 hours, cooking on a low heat. Turn the pieces of meat and baste every 20 minutes. If need be, add more stock. When the meat is ready add the grated lemon rind (only the yellow part) and the parsley. Turn the heat down for 5 minutes so the meat absorbs the flavour of the lemon rind. Serve on a bed of *risotto alla Milanese* or mashed potato.

Pollo alla Marengo
(chicken in brandy and tomatoes)

After the Austrian army was defeated at Marengo, south of Piedmont, Napoleon invited his victorious generals to a celebration dinner. As Dunan, his chef, had very little in the pantry he had to make do with what he had, and this is what he threw together.

4 chicken pieces	150g (6oz) mushrooms
500g (1lb) fresh peeled plum tomatoes (or a tin peeled tomatoes)	4 slices white bread
	3 tablespoons chopped fresh parsley
½ lemon	100ml (4floz) vegetable oil
60g (2oz) flour	2 tablespoons brandy
60g (2oz) butter	Salt and pepper to taste
1 garlic clove	
150ml (¼ pint) chicken stock	

Wash and dry the chicken pieces, squeeze a lemon over them and coat them evenly in flour. Take a large frying pan, heat the oil and brown the pieces on both sides (about 10 minutes). Remove the chicken (put the pan on one side as you will need it later) and put the pieces in a saucepan with half the butter. If you have bought fresh tomatoes, take the skin off by soaking them for 2 minutes in boiling water, then chop them up and add them to the chicken joints together with the chopped clove of garlic, the brandy, chicken stock and the salt and pepper. Cover and simmer over a low heat for about an hour.

Test the chicken to see if it is ready by pricking a leg with a sharp knife (if the juice that comes out is clear, it is ready), then sprinkle on the parsley and stir. Five minutes before serving, fry the mushrooms in the frying pan you used for the chicken, and add them to the chicken. Cut the slices of bread in half and fry them in the remaining oil. Put the fried bread on a large serving dish and pour over the chicken and the sauce.

Pollo tonnato
(cold chicken with a tuna fish sauce)

This is an unusual dish from Lombardy in that it combines meat with fish. Veal is more commonly used but it is just as delicious with cold chicken.

1 medium chicken	*2 anchovy fillets*
3 celery sticks	*1 lemon*
3 carrots	*1 tablespoon capers*
1 large onion	*Mayonnaise (Calve is a good*
200g (7oz) tin drained tuna	*brand)*
fish	*Salt to taste*

Cover the chicken with water and bring to boil. Skim, add the chopped vegetables and simmer for about 1 hour with the lid on. Take the chicken out of the soup and allow it to cool. This stock can be used for a number of other recipes. When the chicken is cool, remove the skin and bones and cut into small pieces. To make the sauce, put the tuna and anchovy fillets into a bowl with the vegetables from the soup and mash it all up with the mayonnaise. Then add a ladleful at a time of the soup to make it thinner, plus the lemon juice. The sauce should be fairly liquid.

Arrange the pieces of chicken on a flat dish so that there are no gaps and pour the sauce over until the chicken is covered. Garnish with capers and serve.

Polpette al limone
(lemon flavoured meatballs)

This is an unusual and simple way to prepare minced beef. The lemon meatballs should be served with mashed potato and a lightly boiled fresh vegetable; garnish with parsley and slices of lemon.

400g (14oz) minced beef
A lemon (another if you
   want to garnish)
100ml (4floz) milk
3 tablespoons freshly grated
   Parmesan cheese

30g (1oz) approximately,
   butter
60g (2oz) breadcrumbs

Take a large bowl and put the minced beef into it with the milk, grated cheese and a pinch of salt. Mix together with a wooden spoon. With your hands, break a piece of the meat off and roll it in your palms to make a walnut-sized ball. Melt the butter in a frying pan. In the meantime put the freshly grated breadcrumbs onto a plate and roll the meatballs in them; put them in the frying pan and cook on a medium heat. After 5 minutes add the juice of a lemon and let it evaporate on a low heat for about 8 minutes, turning the meatballs regularly. Remove from the heat and serve.

Polpettone alla casalinga (meat loaf)

A useful dish for feeding a family, you can add a plain tomato sauce and serve it hot with vegetables, or eat it cold, sliced with a salad.

50g (1lb) minced beef
250g (8oz) minced pork
4 slices of bread
2 eggs
100g (4oz) freshly grated
   Parmesan

2 tablespoons freshly
   chopped parsley
900ml (1½ pints) meat
   stock
Nutmeg
Salt and pepper to taste

Put the minced meat into a large bowl with the eggs and mix well. Soak the slices of bread in a little meat stock and add to the mixture. Sprinkle on a little grated nutmeg, the parsley and season. Roll the meat onto a flat surface and pat into a firm loaf-shape. Transfer it to a greased ovenproof dish and pour over the meat stock. Cover and put it in a preheated oven for about 1 hour. Baste every 20 minutes and turn it over half way through.

Saltimbocca alla Romana (veal parcels with ham and sage)

Saltimbocca literally means 'jump in the mouth'. The dish comes from Rome but *saltimbocca* are eaten all over Italy.

8 thin slices of veal scaloppine	60g (2oz) mozzarella
4 slices of ham or pancetta	100ml (4floz) dry white wine
8 fresh sage leaves	8 toothpicks
60g (2oz) butter	Salt and pepper to taste

Ask the butcher to flatten eight thin slices of veal *scaloppine*. Cut them into wide strips (about 3 inches wide) or big enough to make little parcels. Cut the ham to approximately the same sizes. Sprinkle a little salt and pepper on each piece of veal, put the ham on top of the meat with a small piece of cheese and a fresh sage leaf. Roll the meat into a little parcel and secure it with a toothpick so it doesn't unravel. Put the butter in the frying pan and when it has turned pale brown, add the meat rolls. When the meat is golden brown on all sides, pour on the wine, cover and let it simmer on a low heat for about 20 minutes. Remove from the heat and serve immediately.

Scaloppine ammantate
(veal escalopes with *mozzarella*)

A simple dish, with melted *mozzarella* cheese on top.

180g (6oz) mozzarella cheese	45g (1½oz) butter
700g (1½lb) scaloppine of veal (or four pieces sliced very thinly)	2 tablespoonfuls of oil
	Salt and pepper

Make sure the veal is flattened and nick the edges to prevent them curling up. Slice the *mozzarella* into the same number of pieces as you have meat. Pick the biggest frying pan you have and heat the butter and oil until almost smoking. When it stops foaming add the meat and brown on both sides (about 1 minute). Season with salt and turn the heat down. Place a piece of *mozzarella* on top of each piece of meat, add pepper and cover until the cheese melts. Serve immediately. Scrape the pan and add a few spoons of water to make a quick sauce.

Trippa alla Livornese
(tripe in oil and vinegar)

They eat a lot of tripe in Italy, especially in the north, and often with *polenta*. It is cheap, has a slightly sweet taste, so needs quite a lot of herbs or pepper in cooking. This is one of the lesser known recipes.

1 kg (2¼lb) tripe
4 tablespoons olive oil
1 tablespoon wine vinegar
3 tablespoons freshly
  chopped parsley

Salt and freshly ground
  black pepper

Rinse the tripe several times in cold water. Fill a large saucepan two-thirds full of water, add a pinch of salt and bring to the boil. Cut the tripe into 2-inch wide strips and put into the boiling water. Lower the heat and cook, covered, for 2 hours. Drain the tripe in a colander or strainer and set aside. Pour the olive oil into the saucepan you have just used, add the tripe, season and leave for 2 minutes. Take a deep prewarmed dish and put in the tripe. Pour the vinegar into the pan and let it heat up, then pour it over the ready-to-serve dish and mix well. Sprinkle parsley on top.

DESSERTS

Coppe di melone e anguria
(melon and watermelon salad)

This is a very pretty and summery dish which is easy to prepare.

2 small ripe round melons
½ watermelon
30g (1 oz) sugar

Cognac, optional, 2
tablespoons

Cut the two small melons in half horizontally and with a teaspoon remove all the pips.

Gouge out little balls of melon pulp with a scoop or teaspoon and put them in a bowl. Keep the melon shells intact, but scoop away most of the flesh and put the juice in the bowl with the melon balls. Do the same with the watermelon. Sprinkle the sugar over the yellow and red melon balls and add the cognac if you want. Mix together and put the multicoloured balls back into the melon shells. Put them in the fridge and serve cold.

Crema di ricotta
(cream of *ricotta* cheese)

This is a very quick and simple dessert. The *ricotta* must be fresh. Children love it with a little sugar and cinnamon sprinkled over it.

300g (10oz) ricotta
150ml (¼ pint) cream
180g (6oz) white sugar

3 teaspoons cocoa powder
(or instant coffee)
3 tablespoons vodka
(optional)

Whisk the *ricotta*, cream, sugar and the vodka in a bowl. If you have a blender, so much the better, if not use a fork. Whisk until it becomes a frothy cream and then pour it into four individual tall glasses. Put them in the fridge for at least half an hour. Just before serving sprinkle on the cocoa powder or instant coffee.

Fichi al forno
(baked figs)

Desserts made with fruit are not only easy to prepare, but

delicious in the summer months when Italy has such a wide variety to choose from. This is an unusual way to serve figs, you can use either the green or the dark purple variety and they must be ripe and thin-skinned.

12 figs   *60g (2oz) butter*
60g (2oz) sugar   *Rind from ½ lemon*

Wash the figs carefully. Put the sugar in a small bowl and roll each fig in it so it has an even coating. Take an ovenproof dish and grease it well inside with the butter, then place the figs upright in the dish so they are packed in and touching. Pour three tablespoons of cold water over the figs and add the finely chopped rind from half a lemon. Put the figs in the oven on a medium heat for 10 minutes so the sugar becomes caramellised. When the dish has cooled down, put it in the fridge. The figs should be served very cold.

Granita di caffè con panna
(crushed coffee ice with cream)

This is a light, refreshing dessert to end any meal and is also delicious at teatime.

200g (7oz) white sugar   *¼ litre (½ pint) sugared*
½ litre (¾ pint) water   *whipped cream*
6 small espresso cups of
*   strong black coffee*

Put the sugar, coffee and water in a saucepan and heat until the sugar has dissolved. Remove and let it cool. Pour the coffee into two freezer trays (ice-cube trays) and put them in the freezer for 1 hour. Take them out and smash up the iced coffee and put it back in the trays in the freezer. Repeat after another hour and pour the crushed ice into tall wine glasses, add a dollop of cream on top and serve.

Le bisse
(snake-shaped biscuits)

Le bisse in Venetian dialect means water snakes, hence the S shape. These biscuits are very easy to make. If you want to make more than the suggested amount, just double all the ingredients, stick to the measurements fairly carefully or the biscuits can turn out as heavy as lead!

3 eggs
180g (6oz) white sugar
150ml (¼ pint) vegetable
  oil

6 walnuts (or any other nut)
550g (1lb 2oz) plain flour
A pinch of salt

Take a large bowl, put in the sugar and break in the eggs. Mix with a wooden spoon until pale and creamy. Crack and peel the nuts (put the nuts in boiling water for 1 minute, so the skins will come away easily), chop them up and add them to the mixture. Pour in the oil, the flour and a pinch of salt. Knead thoroughly. Put the dough in some clingfilm or a damp cloth and place in the fridge for an hour. Grease a large baking tray. Take a little ball of dough and roll it between your palms to make a 'snake' about 4 inches (10cm) long. Place it on the tray in an S shape. When you have used all the dough put the tray in a hot oven for about 4 or 5 minutes and then turn the heat down for another 15 minutes until the biscuits are golden brown.

Pere ripiene
(pears stuffed with *Gorgonzola*)

This is a delicious savoury/sweet combination using one of Italy's most delicious cheeses — a speciality of Milan.

4 ripe eating pears
60g (2oz) Gorgonzola
30g (1oz) unsalted butter
2½ teaspoons lemon juice

2 tablespoons crushed nuts:
  pistachios or pine kernels
  and walnuts

Peel the pears if they are the tough skinned variety, otherwise leave on the skins after washing. Cut lengthways leaving the stem attached to one of the halves. Core and scoop out about two teaspoonfuls of the fruit. If you've peeled them, paint with the lemon juice to stop discolouring.

Put the *Gorgonzola* and the butter in a bowl. Both should have been left out of the fridge and be fairly soft. Mix them together with a wooden spoon until soft and creamy, fill the holes in the pears with the mixture and press firmly together. Roll the pears in the chopped nuts. Choose a dish in which they can stand upright, stalks uppermost and chill for two hours to harden the cheese.

Pesche al vino rosso
(peaches in red wine)

Italians eat few puddings but lots of fruit. They love to soak their fruit in wine. This is a delicious and easy recipe for peaches.

6 ripe but unblemished
   peaches
6 teaspoons sugar
Rind of ½ lemon

300ml (10fl oz) dry red wine
   (Chianti would be ideal)

Wash and dry the peaches. Cut them in half lengthways and remove the stones and then cut into thin slices. Put them, unpeeled (the skin is tender) into a deep bowl and sprinkle with sugar. Take the rind from half a lemon (just the yellow part), chop it up and sprinkle over the peaches. Cover the peaches with the red wine and leave overnight in a cool place, but don't refrigerate. They look best served in tall glasses with the wine in which they were marinated.

Torta di marroni
(chestnut cake)

This is a rich and easy cake to make — a little slice goes a long way and it doesn't need cooking. It's best made 24 hours in advance, kept in the fridge and served cold. You can buy jars of chestnut purée much cheaper in Italy than here. If you don't want to make it while you're away, you can always bring a few home.

400g jar of chestnut purée
   (crema di marroni)
120g (4oz) butter
2 packets sponge fingers
   (savoiardi biscuits)

120g (4oz) plain chocolate
125ml (5fl oz) strong coffee
1 tablespoon of brandy, rum
   or any other liqueur
Mascarpone cream to top

Put the chocolate in a glass bowl and melt by placing it in a pan of boiling water (off the heat and not touching the bottom). Cream the butter and add the chocolate to it, work in the chestnut purée. Grease a 2lb-loaf tin or a round tin about 8 inches wide by 3 inches (or anything else you have). Divide the sponge fingers into three groups, dip them one at a time into the hot coffee and brandy and lay one group at the bottom of the dish. Add half the purée, another layer of sponge fingers, the rest of the purée and finish with sponge fingers. If they have already soaked up all the coffee and brandy, make a little more. Finish with blobs of *mascarpone* cream.

Glossaries

SHOPPING WORDS AND PHRASES

A kilo of …	*Un chilo di*
A piece of that one	*Un pezzo di quelli*
Can I pay with this credit card?	*Posso pagare con questa carta di credito?*
Do you accept travellers' cheques?	*Accettate i travellers' cheques?*
Excuse me	*Mi scusi*
Good afternoon/evening	*Buona sera*
Good morning	*Buon giorno*
Goodbye	*Arriverderci*
Half a kilo	*Mezzo chilo*
Have you any …?	*Ha…/avete?*
Hello	*Ciao*
How much is … this/that?	*Quanto costa?* *Questo/Quello*
I don't speak Italian	*Io non parlo Italiano*
I don't understand	*Non capisco*
I want to buy	*Vorrei comprare*
I'd like some	*Vorrei*
It's too expensive	*È troppo caro*
Large	*Grande*
Please	*Per favore*
Please give me	*Per favore mi dia*
Small	*Piccolo*
Thank you	*Grazie*
What is this?	*Cos'è questo?*
Where do they sell?	*Dove vendono?*
Will you deliver it?	*Lo potete consegnare a domicilio?*

HERBS, STAPLES AND SUNDRIES

Anchovies	*Alici, acciughe*
Bay leaves	*Foglie d'alloro*
Basil	*Basilico*
Beans	*Fagioli*

Beer	*Birra*
Borage	*Boraggine*
Bread	*Pane*
Breadcrumbs	*Pangrattato*
Butter	*Burro*
Cheese	*Formaggio*
Chicken	*Pollo*
Cinnamon	*Cannella*
Cloves	*Chiodi di garofano*
Coffee	*Caffè*
Coriander	*Coriandolo*
Cream	*Panna, crema*
Eggs	*Uova*
Fennel seeds	*Semi di finocchio*
Fish	*Pesce*
Flour	*Farina*
Juniper	*Ginepro*
Marjoram	*Origano*
Matches	*Cerini/fiammiferi*
Meat	*Carne*
Milk	*Latte*
Mint	*Menta*
Myrtle	*Mirto*
Nutmeg	*Noce moscata*
Oil	*Olio*
Olive oil	*Olio d'oliva*
Olives	*Olive*
Parsley	*Prezzemolo*
Pepper	*Pepe*
Pine nuts	*Pinoli*
Rice	*Riso*
Rocket	*Rucola, ravanelli*
Rosemary	*Rosmarino*
Saffron	*Zafferano*
Sage	*Salvia*
Salt	*Sale*
Semolina	*Semolino*
Thyme	*Timo*
Tunny fish	*Tonno in scatola*
Vinegar	*Aceto*
Wine	*Vino*

MEAT, POULTRY AND GAME

Beef	*Manzo*
Chicken	*Pollo*

Duck	*Anatra*
Goose	*Oca*
Hare	*Lepre*
Kid	*Capretto*
Lamb	*Agnello*
baby lamb	*Abbacchio*
Oxtail	*Coda alla vaccinara*
Partridge	*Pernice*
Pigeon	*Piccione*
Pork	*Maiale*
suckling pig	*Porchetta*
Quail	*Quaglia*
Rabbit	*Coniglio*
Small birds	*Uccelli*
Turkey	*Tacchino*
Veal	*Vitello*
Venison	*Cervo*
Wild boar	*Cinghiale*

MEAT PRODUCTS

Bacon	*Pancetta affumicata*
Blade (shoulder)	*Spalla*
Brains	*Cervello*
Breast	*Petto di*
Chops	*Nodini* (veal), *braciola*
Cutlets	*Costoletta*
Escalopes	*Scaloppine/piccate*
Fillet	*Filetti*
Game	*Cacciagione*
Ham cooked	*Prosciutto cotto*
Ham raw	*Prosciutto crudo*
Heart	*Cuore*
Kidneys	*Rognoni*
Leg (lamb)	*Gamba (cosciotto) d'agnello*
Leg (pork)	*Prosciutto (cosciotto) di maiale*
Liver	*Fegato*
Loin	*Lombata*
Pate	*Pate*
Pork products	*Salumi*
Poultry	*Pollame*
Rib (beef)	*Costa di manzo, costola*
Rib (veal)	*Costa di vitello*
Roast beef	*Arrosto di manzo*

Salami	*Salame*
Sausages	*Salsicce*
Shoulder	*Spalla*
Steak	*Bistecca*
Sweetbreads	*Animelle di vitello*
Tongue	*Lingua*
Topside, top rump	*Fesa, fettine di manzo*
Tripe	*Trippa*

Phrases

A bigger piece please	*Mi può dare un pezzo più grande*
A smaller piece please	*Mi può dare un pezzo più piccolo*
I would like … kilos of	*Vorrei … chili di …*
Please bone it	*Può dissossarlo*
Please cut it	*Può tagliarlo*
Please flatten it	*Può batterlo/a*
Please mince it	*Può macinarla*
Please slice it	*Può affetarlo*

FISH

Anchovies	*Alici, acciughe*
Angler	*Rana pescatrice*
Bream	*Dentice, orata*
Brill	*Rombo liscio*
Eel	*Anguilla*
Flounder	*Passera pianuzza*
Garfish	*Aguglia*
Grey mullet	*Cefalo, dorato*
Grouper	*Cernia*
John Dory	*Pesce san Pietro*
Ray	*Razza*
Red mullet	*Triglie*
Salt cod	*Baccalà*
Sardines	*Sarde*
Sea bass	*Spigola*
Smooth hound	*Palombo*
Sole	*Sogliola*
Swordfish	*Pesce spada*
Trout	*Trota*
Tuna	*Tonno*

Shellfish and Molluscs

Clams	*Vongole*
Crab	*Granchio*
Crawfish	*Astice, aragostine*
Cuttlefish	*Seppie*
Date shell	*Dattero di mare*
Lobster	*Aragosta, astice*
Mantis shrimps	*Cannocchie*
Mussels	*Cozze*
Octopus	*Polipi*
Oysters	*Ostriche*
Prawns	*Gamber (ell)i*
Scallops	*Canestrelli*
Scampi	*Scampi*
Sea urchins	*Ricci di mare*
Shrimps	*Gamberetti*
Squid	*Calamari*

Phrases

I would like … kilos of	*Vorrei … chili di …*
Can you clean it?	*Può pulire?*

VEGETABLES

Artichokes	*Carciofi*
Asparagus	*Asparagi*
Aubergines/Eggplant	*Melanzane*
Beetroot	*Barbabietole*
Broad beans	*Fave*
Broccoli	*Broccoli*
Cabbage	*Cavolo*
Cardoons	*Cardi*
Cauliflower	*Cavolfiori*
Celery	*Sedano*
Chard	*Biete*
Chicory	*Cicoria*
Courgette/Zucchini	*Zucchini*
Cucumber	*Cetrioli*
Fennel	*Finocchio*
French beans	*Fagiolini verdi*
Garlic	*Aglio*
Jerusalem artichokes	*Topinambur*
Lamb's lettuce	*Pasqualina*
Mushrooms	*Funghi*
Onions	*Cipolle*
Peas	*Piselli*

Peppers	*Peperoni*
Potatoes	*Patate*
Radishes	*Ravanelli*
Salad	*Insalata*
Salsify	*Sassefrica*
Spinach	*Spinaci*
Tomatoes	*Pomodori*
Truffles	*Tartufi*

FRUIT

Apples	*Mele*
Apricots	*Albicocche*
Banana	*Banana*
Cherries	*Ciliege*
Figs	*Fichi*
Grapes	*Uva*
Lemons	*Limoni*
Loquats	*Nespole*
Melons	*Meloni*
Nectarines	*Pesche noce*
Oranges	*Arance*
Peaches	*Pesche*
Pears	*Pere*
Persimmon	*Cacchi/kaki*
Plums	*Susine*
Pomegranates	*Melagrani*
Prickly pear	*Fichi d'India*
Raspberries	*Lamponi*
Strawberries	*Fragole*
Watermelon	*Cocomero, anguria*

NUTS

Almonds	*Mandorle*
Chestnuts	*Castagne, marrone*
Hazelnuts	*Nocciole*
Pinenuts	*Pinoli*
Walnuts	*Noci*

NUMBERS

Nought	*Zero*
One	*Uno*
Two	*Due*
Three	*Tre*
Four	*Quattro*
Five	*Cinque*
Six	*Sei*
Seven	*Sette*
Eight	*Otto*
Nine	*Nove*
Ten	*Dieci*
Eleven	*Undici*
Twelve	*Dodici*
Thirteen	*Tredici*
Fourteen	*Quattordici*
Fifteen	*Quindici*
Sixteen	*Sedici*
Seventeen	*Diciassette*
Eighteen	*Diciotto*
Nineteen	*Diciannove*
Twenty	*Venti*
Thirty	*Trenta*
Forty	*Quaranta*
Fifty	*Cinquanta*
Sixty	*Sessanta*
Seventy	*Settanta*
Eighty	*Ottanta*
Ninety	*Novanta*
One hundred	*Cento*
One thousand	*Mille*
Five thousand	*Cinquemila*
Ten thousand	*Diecimila*
Fifty thousand	*Cinquantamila*
One hundred thousand	*Centomila*
One million	*Un milione*

Weights and Measures

The following tables of solid and liquid measures are approximate.

SOLID

Ounces	Grams
1/2	15
1	30
2	60
2½	75
3½	100 (etto)
4	120
6	180
8	250
10	300
1 lb	500
2¼ lb	1 kg
3 lb	1½ kg

LIQUID

British Imperial	Metric
1 fl oz	25 ml
2 fl oz	50 ml
3 fl oz	75 ml
4 fl oz	100 ml
5 fl oz	125 ml
8 fl oz	225 ml
½ pint	300 ml
1 pint	600 ml
American	*Metric*
1 fl oz	30 ml
2 fl oz	60 ml
3 fl oz	90 ml
4 fl oz	120 ml
5 fl oz	150 ml
½ pint	240 ml
1 pint	480 ml

OVEN TEMPERATURES

	Centigrade	Gas	Fahrenheit
Very cool	130°C	½	250°F
Cool	150°C	2	300°F
Warm	170°C	3	325°F
Moderate	180°C	4	350°F
Fairly hot	190°C	5	375°F
	200°C	6	400°F
Hot	220°C	7	425°F
Very hot	230°C	8	450°F

Bibliography

Belfrage, Nicolas *Life Beyond Lambrusco* (Sidgwick & Jackson, 1985)

Berlitz *Italian for Travellers* (and regional guides) (Berlitz, 1986)

Bugialli, Giuliano *The Taste of Italy* (Conran Octopus, 1984)

David, Elizabeth *Italian Food* (Penguin, 1977)

Davidson, Alan *Mediterranean Seafood* (Penguin, Harmondsworth, 1972)

Del Conte, Anna *Good Housekeeping Italian Cookery* (Ebury Press, 1982)

Del Conte, Anna *Portrait of Pasta* (Paddington Press, 1976)

Hazan, Marcella *The Classic Italian Cookbook* (Papermac, 1981)

Hazan, Marcella *The Second Italian Classic Cookbook* (Papermac, 1983)

Hazan, Victor *Italian Wine* (Penguin, 1982)

Grigson, Jane *Jane Grigson's Vegetable Book* and *Jane Grigson's Fruit Book* (Penguin, 1980, 1982)

Ross, Janet and Waterfield, Michael *Leaves from Our Tuscan Kitchen* (Penguin, 1973)

Scaravelli, Paola and Cohen, Jon *Cooking from an Italian Garden* (Thorsons, 1984)

Sharman, Fay and Chadwick, Brian *The Taste of Italy — Dictionary of Food and Wine* (Papermac, 1985)

The Cooking of Italy (Time Life, 1969)

OTHER SOURCES OF INFORMATION

Italian State Tourist Office
1 Princes Street
London W1R 8AY
Tel: 01-408 1254

Italian Government Travel Office (ENIT)
630 Fifth Avenue
New York, NY
Tel: 212-245-4822

Index

INDEX

INDEX